The Glory in Waiting

When God does not move according
to your schedule

Ursula Lett Robinson

Ursula Lett Robinson
United States of America

Copyright © 2024 Ursula Lett Robinson
All Rights Reserved.

This book has been published with all reasonable efforts taken to make the material error-free after the consent of the author. No part of this book shall be used, reproduced in any manner whatsoever without written permission from the author, except in the case of brief quotations embodied in critical articles and reviews.

The Author of this book is solely responsible and liable for its content including but not limited to the views, representations, descriptions, statements, information, opinions, and references. The Content of this book shall not constitute or be construed or deemed to reflect the opinion or expression of the Publisher or Editor. Neither the Publisher nor Editor endorse or approve the Content of this book or guarantee the reliability, accuracy or completeness of the Content published herein and do not make any representations or warranties of any kind, express or implied, including but not limited to the implied warranties of merchantability, fitness for a particular purpose. The Publisher and Editor shall not be liable whatsoever for any errors, omissions, whether such errors or omissions result from negligence, accident, or any other cause or claims for loss or damages of any kind, including without limitation, indirect or consequential loss or damage arising out of use, inability to use, or about the reliability, accuracy or sufficiency of the information contained in this book.

Dedication

To my mother, Ellen Lett, my first teacher and example of a godly woman, you loved us and modeled and lived Christ in front of us. You taught us how to be godly women and to maintain a godly household. The Proverbs 31 woman, that is who you were. We are blessed; we are grateful.

To my father, Ernest Lett, the epitome of a hardworking family man. Because of you, I had my first natural glimpse of the love of the Heavenly Father.

To my sister, Ivy Lett, you are the personification of grace under fire. I am honored to be your sister.

To my husband, Maurice Robinson, your love makes me smile. Thank you for loving me.

Acknowledgments

So many people have helped me on this journey of writing this book. I want to thank my church family, Priestly Praise Ministries, for their love and support. Special thanks to my Pastor, Apostle Lee Lyons, who prophesied the title of the book to me in 2006. Thank you to Elder Rosalyn Miller and Elder Jeremy Rutland for always asking about my progress on the book. The Holy Spirit used both of you to gently convict me and get me to the place to write and to complete the assignment. Thank you, Elder Annette Brown, for your prayers and your investment in me, I am eternally grateful.

Sister Scribes, words cannot express your importance to me. The sisterhood and camaraderie are unparalleled. This is God's doing, and it is marvelous in my sight. I love you all and am excited about what God is releasing in the earth realm through each of you. I'm absolutely thrilled to be named among you.

Special thanks to Chanel Martin and the Beyond the Book Publishing family and Dr. Monique Rodgers and Shooting Star Publishing for helping me bring the vision to reality.

Table of Contents

Letter from the Author

In III John 3:2 (KJV), the elder (John) writes to Gaius and says, "Beloved, I wish above all things that thou mayest prosper and be in health even as thy soul prospers." Euodoō is the Greek word that is translated as prosper in this verse. This word is a combination of the prefix ευ which means good or well, and the word ὁδός, which is interpreted as journey. John is wishing Gaius well on his journey. It is no different than if you said hello and asked me how my family was doing. So, in context, John is saying that he is praying that Gaius is doing well on his Christian journey. This book is birthed out of the path or road that I took, my journey.

On my journey, I have gone through stages and phases of waiting. I can literally see myself in every chapter. Sometimes, especially in my early walk with the Lord, I was good at waiting. I was young, passionate about the things of God, in good health, and surrounded by other kindred spirits. My career was great, ministry was my life, and all was right with my world.

However, as the saying goes, "everything must change, nothing stays the same." I found that to be true for me. When I was 25 years old, I started having severe back problems with sciatic pain and weakness in both legs. Once vibrant and very athletic, I was now relegated to the sidelines of any and every activity. I experienced chronic and acute pain daily. Pain of that magnitude wears on the mind and soul. I began to isolate myself because I did not want others to see me so weak. I often went home, collapsed on my couch, and just cried. I prayed. Others prayed. We all believed for my healing, but the truth was, the longer the wait, the heavier was the weight of waiting.

Thankfully, I had three examples of perseverance: my mother, Ellen Lett, my pastor, Helena Barrington, and my elder and mentor, Mary Colson-Clayton. These three women loved God, loved their families, and did the work of ministry, all while navigating through chronic pain. These virtuous women exemplified Christ and did not grumble and complain about their respective "thorns in the flesh," but rather, they continued to serve God in excellence and reflect Christ to their families, the Kingdom of God, and the community at large. Even with their examples before me, I struggled to maintain hope of healing.

When I was younger, time was not an issue. However, now it was noticeable, the clock was ticking. I had health problems, the single woman with no worries was now beginning to worry that I would be undesirable. Who would want to marry me, and I already had health issues? I buried myself in church work for two reasons: (1) I loved God and His people, and (2) I didn't have to deal with my emotions if I was too busy and then too tired to cope.

In this stage of life, I developed a weight problem while waiting on God. Did He hear me? Did He see me? Did He care? The answer was an emphatic YES, He did! However, the better question is: Was I listening, looking, and casting my cares on Him in faith? The answer was complicated! Yes and No. I could hear Him, especially when it concerned someone or something else, but I no longer listened to see if He was answering my prayers regarding me. Instead of being honest with Him, I started to stuff my feelings with food. If I didn't deal with the lingering questions, I could continue to fake it. I believed God could do it for others, but I was losing faith that He would do it for me. Yet, God is faithful! If we wait on Him and do so in faith, He does answer, and His answer is always on time.

I learned a lot about myself during the wait. Did I always wait on Him the correct way? No, I didn't. Nevertheless, He didn't give up on me; He wooed me with His loving kindness and His tender mercies. When I had given up on the dream of marriage, he sent my husband. When I had settled for living with health issues, He began the healing process. Over two years (2017-2019), I had 11 total surgeries. God gave me a makeover from head to toe. I am in better health now than when I was in my 30's. Romans 8:28 (NKJV) became real to me: "And we know that all things work together for good to those who love God, to those who are the called according to His purpose."

I learned that there is glory in waiting. Divine order releases divine glory! God does not release his glory in chaos; He is a God of order. Consequently, if we want success, if we want to see God move in our lives, we must submit to His sovereignty, His authority, His plan, and His will.

When we submit to Him, the glory in waiting is revealed in God's stamp of approval on our response to His sovereignty! His stamp of approval will come in the form of the promised child, the unlikely promotion, the total restoration of health, wealth, or relationships, the fulfillment of the dream.

THE GLORY IN WAITING

This devotional is written from my life experiences. Like David, Abraham and Sarah, Hannah, and Elizabeth, the time between the promise and the fulfillment of that promise allowed me time to grow in my faith, to grow in Him. There is glory in waiting on God. Trust me. He is worth the wait.

Introduction

Wait on the LORD; Be of good courage, And He shall strengthen your heart; Wait, I say, on the LORD!

PSALM 27:14 (NKJV)

What do you think of when you hear the word *wait*? Does wait for you mean that you are standing in one spot frantically looking for something or expecting someone? Does waiting mean that progress has stopped for you, that there is no forward movement? Is it just killing time, meaning it is an unproductive time or season in your life? Perhaps waiting for you means that you are in a holding pattern with no ability to move forward until you are released to do so, like an airplane pilot waiting for permission from the air traffic controller to land. Waiting for you may involve expectation, such as holding your breath as one who waits with bated breath. Sometimes the anticipation of a thing (good or bad) will truly have you holding your breath. Or maybe waiting for you means to be anxious, fretful, or full of anxiety? Do you pace the floor, bite your nails, shake your leg, or breathe in a manner that you risk hyperventilation?

You may be one of the few who first thinks of serving others when you think of waiting. Waiting, by definition, can involve all the above. Of the iterations of wait, two things we don't want are (1) to be guilty of being unproductive by "killing time" and (2) to be guilty of a wait filled with anxiety and negative emotions.

Waiting can be dreadful. Waiting can also be pleasurable or peaceful. Waiting doesn't have to be tortuous, even if the event or the news you are waiting for may not be good. The difference is in your attitude and perspective. Trust God in all situations that He will do what is best for you in each and every circumstance. The dilemma becomes, how do I wait so that I receive the benefits of waiting and not the frustrations?

In my short life on this earth, I have experienced each "wait" described above. Sometimes, I got it right, and truthfully, most times, I got it wrong. I wanted to please God and started the race like a sprinter, only to find out this thing called life is a marathon. The training for sprinters is significantly different than the training for long-distance runners.

Training for sprinters involves exercises that enhance their pace and strength. Sprinters will work on coming out of the blocks in bursts of speed and power. Sprinters must learn to stay in their lane or risk disqualification. The runner must get to top speed quickly and maintain it until the finish line. The workout regime, diet, exercise, and mental preparation may go on for several months, but the race will only last for seconds.

Conversely, the training for long-distance runners involves exercises that develop endurance and cardiovascular exercises designed to build lung strength. Runners learn pacing, running at a tempo that they can maintain without draining all their energy, and still have energy for a "kick" as they near the end of the course. The kick requires the runner to muster strength, pick up the pace, and treat the end of the race like a sprint. Long-distance runners, especially those who run marathons, may experience fatigue, dehydration, and cramping while running. Sometimes, at the point of exhaustion, it appears that they will not be able to finish the race, but the runners experience a second wind. When runners get a second wind, they experience a burst of energy that enables them to push past the exhaustion and the pain or discomfort and go the distance and finish the race.

As with the sprinter, the long-distance runner's workout routine, diet, exercise, and mental preparation may last several months. The mental stressors are different for those who run long distances. The long-distance runner does not have to maintain a lane, but he or she must be able to run in a pack or alone. Whether a sprinter or a long-distance runner, both must focus on their goal, the finish line.

Paul used a running analogy in Galatians 5:7 when he made a statement and asked a question: "you did run well; who did hinder you that you should not obey the truth?" Running the race is only part of the equation. Whether sprinting or running long distances, there are still rules that must be followed for your race and, ultimately, your win to be legitimate. Paul, in this instance, is saying that one cannot run the Christian race and not be guided by the truth of God's Word.

In order to run this race and be guided by truth, we must understand how to wait and how to be of good courage. The promise is realized after a "successful" wait. When the scripture says to be of good courage, exactly what is good courage?

THE GLORY IN WAITING

Courage is the mindset or ability to do something that frightens you. It is the ability to fight something alarming, painful, or grievous. When the psalmist says to "be of good courage," he is admonishing you to grab ahold of that mindset or that ability to fight through the very thing that you are afraid to go through. When you wait on the Lord, wait with expectancy. Wait for the Lord with joy, trusting in Him and knowing that you don't have to be afraid of the outcome.

God has promised that He will strengthen our hearts when we wait on him. Inherent in that promise is the understanding that we must "wait" in the proper manner. No matter your outlook, God has a word for you in the season you find yourself. He longs to make your wait time fruitful and that it be a time of pleasure and personal satisfaction. He desires you to know that waiting on Him is not to torture you but to bless you.

My desire is that you will begin to understand in a fresh way that the blessing is not in the stressing but in the pressing. Waiting on God requires pressing into His presence. When you press (exert effort) into His presence, even though you become fatigued from pressing, He assures you that He will renew your strength, He will grant you everything you need to finish strong. Resolve within yourself that you will wait on God.

I challenge you to journey with me and let us discover together how to wait on the Lord, for there is glory in waiting on Him. This is a devotion and a workbook designed to enhance your spiritual growth. Be honest and transparent with yourself and God as you study each chapter. Take off the mask and be truthful about your feelings and thoughts. God desires to bless you more than you can imagine.

Each chapter ends with prayer, space for writing your reflections, and a declaration. The Hebrew word *achvah* is translated as the English word, "declare," and it means "to make known, to give an accounting of." When you make a declaration, you are voicing and making known in the natural what you are in possession of in the spiritual. A decree is a legally binding document. When we decree, we say that "it is written," and we speak a truth that carries the authority of the court of Heaven. Decrees are the expressed will and purpose of God in any situation. The Hebrew word for decree is *azar*, which means to divide, cut in two, destroy. You are decreeing unlawful anything contrary to the will of God and destroying its power over you, cutting it away or off of you.

So, when you declare, you are stating what you have (spiritually) taken possession of. When you decree, it is the written authority upon which your declaration is voiced. Job 22:28 (AMPC) states, "You shall also decide and decree a thing, and it shall be established for you; and the light [of God's favor] shall shine upon your ways." When we say what God is saying, we will obtain God's favor."

After each chapter, take a few moments and write what you hear the Lord revealing to you about your wait, pray, and then declare what God has decreed about you.

Prayer

Father, we bless Your name, and we honor You right now. We come into Your presence with grateful hearts, and we just want to say thank you for all that You have done for us.

Dear Lord, as we embark on this spiritual journey, open our eyes to see the wonders in Your Word. Open our ears to hear You clearly.

THE GLORY IN WAITING

Touch our hearts to receive You. Cause us to focus on You and to not allow any distractions to draw us from Your presence. We need You, Lord, in every aspect of our lives. As we study about waiting on You, we already know that You have been waiting on us to come to You, waiting on us to spend time with You, waiting on us to yield to You.

Forgive us, Lord, for we have sinned and fallen short of Your glory. Because You are faithful, we know that You have forgiven us, You have cleansed us, and You have declared us righteous. David said in Psalms 51, "create in me a clean heart and renew a right spirit within me." That is our prayer, Lord, that You would purify our hearts and make us new in You.

Daddy God, whatever You desire of us, we will be the people You can depend on. We love You and appreciate You.

Now please, Sir, speak to us, Lord, we are listening. In Jesus' name, I pray. Amen.

Reflections

THE GLORY IN WAITING

Declaration

I declare that I can see what God is saying in my circumstances. I acknowledge that God is in control of everything, and if He has me waiting, then I can wait in expectation that He who began a good work is faithful to complete it in me. I declare that I am the righteousness of God in Christ Jesus and that I can do ALL things through Him who gives me strength. I declare that as it is already decreed in Heaven, it will be fulfilled in me.

Chapter 1

Qavah

But they that wait upon the LORD shall renew their
strength; they shall mount up with wings as eagles; they
shall run, and not be weary.

ISAIAH 40:31 (KJV)

In Isaiah 40:31, the Hebrew word *qavah* is translated as "wait." It means to look eagerly for, to hope, or expect. Like a child standing on tiptoe watching and waiting for their parent to come through the door, the hope is full of joy; it is full of desire. The intensity of the desire infects the attitude and mood of the person. You are waiting, but there is no stress or anxiety in the wait. The thought brings you joy, not dread.

What are you waiting for? Are you waiting for circumstances and situations to change in your life? Are you waiting for a spouse or hoping for children to fill your heart and your home? Maybe you are waiting to be recognized for your excellent work or for being a team player? What are you looking for?

Often, when we are waiting, we are idle, twiddling our thumbs. Or we find something to distract us so that we don't become anxious. We decide that it will not happen for us if we think about it. We play video games or scroll Facebook, Instagram, and Tik Tok when we should be praying and listening to the still small voice of God.

Let's look at the first time qavah is used in the Bible. Genesis 1:9-10, 20a (AMPC)

> 9 And God said, Let the waters under the heavens be collected into one place [of standing], and let the dry land appear. And it was so. 10 God called the dry land Earth, and the accumulated waters He called Seas. And God saw that this was good (fitting, admirable) and He approved it. 20 And God said, Let the waters bring forth abundantly and swarm with living creatures, ...

In this passage, qavah is translated as "be collected." Other translations say, "be gathered together." The waters were collected or gathered and waiting. Isn't that interesting? The waters were waiting. What were the waters waiting for? The waters were waiting for God, waiting for God to speak.

In Psalm 24:1 (KJV), David declared that "The earth is the Lord's, and the fulness thereof; the world, and they that dwell therein. 2 For he hath founded it upon the seas and established it upon the floods." The earth or the land is the Lord's and all it contains, the world or the globe and all its inhabitants. Verse 2 says God has fixed the seas and determined where the rivers and streams would flow. All of creation belongs to God, the cattle on a thousand hills, the mountains and valleys, the potatoes in the ground, the gold, silver, and any other mineral that can be mined. Everything belongs to Him. He is responsible for the creation of it all.

Everything God has created, the plants, animals, earth, and sea, appears to have more sense than man. We run ahead of God or move without Him, but the scriptures say that the waters were waiting in one place, and then God spoke. The waters were located under the heavens. They were placed there by God, and they did not move until God spoke. And when He spoke, He gave the waters the directions that provided a name and their purpose. The accumulated waters were now called seas.

Biblically, a name identifies purpose. The purpose of the seas is found in verse 20. God spoke, and the seas brought forth all manner of marine life in abundance. The waiting produced an ecosystem of sustainable life. The waiting produced abundant life. Do you see that? Abundance was generated through the waiting. If you are experiencing lack or a drought in your life, wait on God. If you wait on God, He will speak to your circumstance, and purpose and abundance will result from your waiting on God.

Inherent and innate in everything God has made is the ability to hear Him and respond, to obey. He made man with free will. Because mankind has free will, we can choose to obey or not. Reflect on your life, on your habits.

The ability to hear God in any circumstance is developed while we wait. Let's look at Elijah for a moment. Elijah was a bold prophet for the Lord. He had just had a great victory over the prophets of Baal. He should be rejoicing, right? But King Ahab told his wife, Jezebel, what Elijah had done, and she sent word to Elijah that she would execute him just like he had executed 450 prophets of Baal and 400 prophets of Asherah. When he heard that Jezebel had put a bounty on his head, he ran. This great man of God now ran for his life. He ran an estimated 335 miles from Mt Carmel to Mt Horeb. In 1 Kings 19:11-13, Elijah has an experience with God, unlike anything he has experienced before.

> ¹¹ Then He said, "Go out, and stand on the mountain before the LORD." And behold, the LORD passed by, and a great and strong wind tore into the mountains and broke the rocks in pieces before the LORD, *but* the LORD *was* not in the wind; and after the wind an earthquake, *but* the LORD *was* not in the earthquake; ¹² and after the earthquake a fire, *but* the LORD *was* not in the fire; and after the fire a still small voice. ¹³ So it was, when Elijah heard *it,* that he wrapped his face in his mantle and went out and stood in the entrance of the cave. Suddenly a voice *came* to him, and said, "What are you doing here, Elijah?"

Elijah waited to hear God speak to him. He saw and felt God as he passed by and tore into the mountains and broke the rocks. He noticed that God was not in that noisy place. He experienced an earthquake, and he noticed that God was not in an unstable event, nor was he in the pressing or the breath-taking fiery situation. It was in the quietness that he heard God. Elijah had to wait on God to speak to him. And when He did, he asked Elijah a simple question, "What are you doing here, Elijah?"

When we quiet our spirits to hear the Lord, He often asks us how we got to this place. Remember, after Adam and Eve sinned,

God asked Adam, "Where are you?" When we are in our feelings or let circumstances and situations get us off focus, God will ask us to identify where we are. Only when we can acknowledge where we are will He then come in and adjust our course.

Are you rushing into or out of situations when you should be waiting on God to speak? Take a moment and listen to Him. You may not hear Him in the hustle and bustle. You may not hear God when your mind is not focused and confusion and uncertainty have set in. If you wait on Him, if you allow yourself to be silent, you will hear Him speak. What does Father God desire of you right now? What is He saying to you right now?

Prayer

Heavenly Father,

I come to You now asking that You forgive me for not waiting on You to come into my circumstances and situations. Forgive me for rushing ahead of You, for making messes. Sometimes I don't even come to You until after I have made the mess bigger.

Father, You said in Your Word, in John 10:5, that Your sheep know Your voice and because we know Your voice, we will not follow a stranger.

Dig my ears, Lord. Clean out any wax build-up that would cause me not to hear You. Father, help me know Your voice. Just as we can recognize another's voice on the telephone without seeing their face, help me recognize Your voice.

I know that You are always with me. You have not ever left me, nor will You ever leave me. Help me to know Your voice when things are going well and when they aren't. Help me to love the sound of Your voice, to listen for You to speak, and to listen intently when You are speaking.

Father, what is it that You desire of me right now? Speak, Lord, I'm listening.

In Jesus' name, I pray. Amen.

Reflections

THE GLORY IN WAITING

Declaration

I wait, expectantly, hopefully, and joyfully for my God and my Lord to speak to me. I declare that by the power of God, I know and understand His voice. I declare that I choose to be obedient, quiet my emotions, and listen. I will listen for the voice of God, and I will not move until I have received His directions. I am His sheep. I will not follow another's voice.

CHAPTER 2

Distracted Service

But Martha was distracted with much serving...

LUKE 10:40A (NKJV)

A secondary meaning of qavah is to bind together and collect, as one who twists or plaits the hair. Plaiting is the technique in which you first part or divide the hair into three even sections. Starting at the scalp, you cross the right section over the middle section and then cross the left section over the middle section intertwining the hair together, continuing this process until you get to the end of the hair, and then you secure the ends. Plaiting the hair puts the hair in a fixed hairstyle. The natural benefit of plaiting the hair is that it is a protective style. Plaiting keeps the hair in place and prevents breakage. Plaiting keeps the hair tamed and manageable. Plaiting hair can lock moisture into the hair that would otherwise be released. When hair is plaited, it is not subject to wind or movement.

They that wait [plait their lives and intertwine their lifestyle into the Lord's plans] shall renew their strength. When your life is plaited into God's purposes and plans, you are protected, you will not be tossed to and fro by every wind and doctrine, chaos will not be your "portion" because He leads you beside the still waters. You experience peace because He is the Prince of Peace.

Are you feeling frazzled, stressed, worn out? Are you just tired in general? If so, could it be that your life is not plaited in the Lord? Just because you are busy doing church work 24/7, 365 does not mean you are fulfilling God's purpose for your life.

Let's look to Martha for clarity on how our lives should be plaited into God.

> [38] Now while they were on their way, it occurred that Jesus entered a certain village, and a woman named Martha received *and* welcomed Him into her house. [39] And she had a sister named Mary, who seated herself at the Lord's feet and was listening to His teaching. [40] But Martha [overly occupied and too busy] was distracted with much serving; and she came up to Him and said, Lord, is it nothing to You that my sister has left me to serve alone? Tell her then to help me [to lend a hand and do her part along with me]!
>
> [41] But the Lord replied to her by saying, Martha, Martha, you are anxious and troubled about many things; [42] There is need of only one *or but* [a]*a few things.* Mary has chosen the good portion [[b]that which is to her advantage], which shall not be taken away from her.
>
> Luke 10:38-42 (AMPC)

THE GLORY IN WAITING

In biblical times, there were no convenience stores, no refrigerators, no microwaves. The typical Hebrew woman's day began at sunrise. The women would get water from the well for the day's cooking. To make their daily bread required planning and forethought over 24 hours; they would need to allow the yeast to activate and ferment in the dough. They cooked, cleaned their homes, washed clothes, cared for and tutored their children, among other daily tasks. They did not have air conditioning, yet daily they used ovens to prepare their meals. Martha could not call her brother and tell him to stop by the store and grab some fried or rotisserie chicken, mashed potatoes, green beans, and sweet tea because they had unexpected guests.

The text indicates that the visit to Martha's home was not planned. Instead of cooking for herself and her siblings, she is now preparing for an additional thirteen people, Jesus and his disciples. At a minimum, she is cooking for sixteen! Martha is feverishly working to ensure that her guests are comfortable and that they would be able to enjoy a meal. Her sister, Mary, her help, was not helping her at all. Mary was sitting at the feet of Jesus, listening to Him teach, just as their guests were doing. When Martha asked Jesus to reprimand Mary, He didn't reprimand Mary but rather gently corrected Martha's perception.

Mary's position, sitting at the feet of Jesus, was that of a student, a disciple. Historically, this posture would be only taken by a man, not a woman. Martha's expectation that she and Mary would be working together was totally reasonable and fit with societal norms. The societal roles were somewhat rigid and unbending. Mary ignored societal norms and sat as one eager to learn from Jesus. Jesus did not discourage Mary.

THE GLORY IN WAITING

Martha was distracted by her serving. She was so focused on what needed to be done and ensuring everything was done timely that she became anxious. Anxiety does not come from God. Philippians 4:6, says "Be anxious for nothing, but in everything by prayer and supplication, with thanksgiving, let your requests be made known to God." Martha's spirit had become sidetracked, preoccupied, unfocused. As a result, she could not even enjoy the presence of Jesus in her home.

Some people get such joy from serving others that they are content, at peace, and happy even though they are working. The task does not dictate their mood, state of mind, or disposition. Life may be handing out lemons, but they are making lemonade with a smile.

When Jesus accepted Martha's invitation, it was never His intention for His visit to be a burden. Martha had invited the one man who could take five fish and two loaves of bread, feed 5,000 and have leftovers. Surely, He could assist her with feeding 16. At the request of his mother, Jesus had taken care of a deficit at a wedding reception by turning water into wine. Experts say it can take three to five years from planting to harvesting and bottling wine. Jesus did, in one moment, what normally takes years to do.

Martha became distracted in her serving. Martha just needed to make her request known to the one who could assist her, Jesus. We can receive instantly from the Father what would normally take years if we would just do like Jesus' mother did and ask in faith believing. Martha, who loved to serve, had lost focus, and instead of enjoying service, she was now frantic, thinking about everything that needed to be done. To be clear, Jesus did not tell Martha to stop working. He just adjusted her vision so that she could see what was important. Mary sitting at the master's feet to hear His teachings was the important thing.

There are the faithful few who can be counted on to do the bulk of the work in every church. Sometimes, they may miss out on sanctuary activities as they work in the kitchen or children's church, the parking and security ministries, etc. God is able to put the same spirit on those working the vision as He has on the visionary. In Numbers 11:16-30, God takes the spirit that is upon Moses and places it on 70 elders in the congregation. In verse 26, we see two of the seventy were still in the camp. "Two men remained in the camp, one named Eldad, and the other named Medad, and the spirit rested on them; they were among those registered, but they had not gone out to the tent, and so they prophesied in the camp." They received the same impartation as those that were in the tent. We don't have to fear missing out on anything. God can impart to those working elsewhere in ministry just as He does the congregation in the sanctuary. We just need to keep our attitude of service pure, and God is faithful to do the rest.

God desires that we plait our life in Him. He wants to be intertwined into our thoughts, actions, our habits, our lifestyles. When plaited, we won't go outside of God to fix the situation. When plaited, we won't wait outside of God or without His presence. When our lives are plaited in God, we avoid danger and breakage. We maintain moisture, so we are pliable in His hands. When plaited, we who are twisted and bound together in God shall renew or restore our strength. Only those who have committed their lives to His purpose will experience the renewing of their strength. Ecclesiastes 4:12 says, "Though one may be overpowered by another, two can withstand him. And a threefold cord is not quickly broken."

The cord that is twisted gains strength or is supported and reinforced by the process of the twisting, the plaiting. We become stronger as our lives are interwoven with God. Instead of weakening us, waiting on the Lord strengthens us.

What has preoccupied you and gotten you off focus? What has you so anxious that you cannot enjoy the presence of God? Take a moment and meditate on Jesus' words in Matthew 11:29-30 (NKJV) "[29] Take My yoke upon you and learn from Me, for I am gentle and lowly in heart, and you will find rest for your souls. [30] For My yoke is easy and My burden is light." If you are like Martha, distracted while serving, take a minute, repent, and then allow God to meet your needs. He's willing, He's able, and He's waiting on you.

Prayer

Dear Heavenly Father,

I come to You asking You to forgive me for allowing distractions to alter my perception of You and Your church. Father, there have been times when I was anxious and fretful, and I didn't believe what You had said. Other times, I became irritated and aggravated, and I did not display Your love, patience, kindness, and character. I was serving, but You could not get the glory because of what I said or did. Sometimes, I said the right things, but my heart was far from it. Forgive me.

I thank You now that because of Your grace and mercy, I have another opportunity to bring You glory and to give You praise in and through my service. May I intertwine my will to Yours and always remember that You will bless me while I am serving in the kitchen, parking the cars, providing security, or cleaning the restroom just like You are blessing those sitting in the sanctuary. Oh God, help me always serve You with a pure and upright heart. I'm Yours, Lord. Do with me what You will. My life is plaited in Yours. In Jesus' name. Amen.

Reflections

THE GLORY IN WAITING

THE GLORY IN WAITING

Declaration

I declare that I have a spirit like Mary because I choose to sit at Your feet and learn of You. I declare that I have a spirit like Martha, seeing the needs and meeting them. I declare that my heart will remain pure and my deeds consecrated to You. I will not misrepresent You in words or deeds. I declare that I am the head and not the tail, above and not beneath. I am more than a conqueror, and I will exceed and excel in every assignment You have entrusted to me. I declare that my strength will be renewed as I plait my life in Yours and serve You and only You.

CHAPTER 3

Do You Want to be Made Well?

Waiting for the moving of the water.

JOHN 5:3B (NKJV)

You have a schedule. You wake up at the same time and prepare yourself for the day. Get your usual breakfast and head out the door for work. Like clockwork, Monday through Friday, you go about your daily routine. No surprises. Your confidence in change occurring is low. Unexpectedly, life throws you a curveball. But you cannot even dare to believe the curveball will be a miracle for you because someone else always beats you to the blessing.

> *¹After this there was a feast of the Jews, and Jesus went up to Jerusalem. ²Now there is in Jerusalem by the Sheep Gate a pool, which is called in Hebrew, Bethesda, having five porches. ³In these lay a great multitude of sick people, blind, lame, paralyzed, waiting for the moving of the water ⁴For an angel went down at a certain time into the pool and stirred up the*

water; then whoever stepped in first, after the stirring of the water, was made well of whatever disease he had. ⁵Now a certain man was there who had an infirmity thirty-eight years. ⁶When Jesus saw him lying there, and knew that he already had been in that condition a long time, He said to him, "Do you want to be made well?" ⁷The sick man answered Him, "Sir, I have no man to put me into the pool when the water is stirred up; but while I am coming, another steps down before me." ⁸Jesus said to him, "Rise, take up your bed and walk." ⁹And immediately the man was made well, took up his bed, and walked. John 5:1-9 (NKJV)

The Greek word translated as "wait" in this passage is ekdechomai, which means to look for, accept from some source, to tarry for. The people were waiting, watching, longing to see the stirring of the water so that they could be the first ones in the water and receive their healing. The man who is the subject of this healing had been inflicted with an infirmity for thirty-eight years. Thirty-eight years of suffering, despair, hope entangled with hopelessness. He is hopeful for healing, so he is at the pool but feels hopeless because he doesn't have anyone to put him in the water if or when it is stirred. He may also be experiencing regret because the text gives us a little insight into the infirmity when Jesus finds the man in the temple after the healing. In verse 14b, Jesus says, "See, you have been made well. Sin no more, lest a worse thing come upon you."

This infirmity, this sickness or disease, was the result of his own actions. In modern times, we might think he has lung cancer from smoking cigarettes, cirrhosis of the liver due to alcoholism, or maybe he contracted a disease through immoral living. When our actions cause our infirmity, we often struggle to receive wholeness because we have a guilty conscience. Jesus knew the man, and He knew the reason for the infirmity. His knowledge did not stop Him from being compassionate. There were a lot of people lying around that pool, but Jesus did not heal everybody that day. In fact, He only focused on one person. Hebrews 4:15 (NKJV) says, "For we do not have a High Priest who cannot sympathize with our weaknesses, but was in all points tempted as we are, yet without sin." The word iniquities is translated in this passage of Scripture as weaknesses.

Everybody has a proclivity, tendency, or weakness for something or someone who is not good. If we don't allow the Holy Spirit to take over in those areas, we will struggle, and more than likely, we will fail. The writer of Hebrews helps us understand that Jesus understands us. He made us; He knows all about us. He has experienced every emotion and tendency that this sinful nature offers, yet the Bible says that although He was tempted, He did not sin. That is the difference between us and Jesus. We are tempted, and we may sin. He was tempted, but He did not sin. This feat qualifies Him to be our savior because He faced the same temptations that we faced, yet He did not sin. Glory to God.

God saw this man's condition, a condition brought on him by his own actions, and Jesus had compassion for Him. God saw the man's heart, and He saw the hindrance to His maintaining the healing. Again, the text gives us a clue in John 5:14. Jesus tells the man that he is whole, to go and live his best life. But He warns the man not to fall or relapse so that he does not experience something more devastating than what Jesus just healed him from.

What thought process might cause an individual to relapse after being healed by Jesus? A guilty conscience. Guilt has driven people who made honest mistakes into doing and saying things that tragically alter the course of their lives. Guilt has driven those who deliberately did wrong into depression or into doing even more evil deeds. Hebrews 10:22 states, "let us draw near with a true heart in full assurance of faith, having our hearts sprinkled from an evil conscience, and our bodies washed with pure water." We must draw near God and allow His Word to clean our minds and memories from an evil, guilty, sinful conscience.

The conscience is the part of you that houses your personality and helps you determine good and evil, right and wrong. Consciousness is the awareness -- or mental and emotional alertness -- to your surroundings. We must lose, or better yet, become desensitized to the sin, the very thing that makes us weak. As the writer in Hebrews admonishes us, in Hebrews 12:1, it is our responsibility to lay aside every weight and the sin that so easily besets us. Besets means to harass, to annoy, to attack. We are responsible for getting rid of the iniquity (weakness) that attacks us.

In 1 John 1:9 (NKJV), John wrote, "If we confess our sins, He is faithful and just to forgive us our sins and cleanse us from all unrighteousness." God will cleanse our guilty conscience, heal us, and make us whole if we confess our sins. Confession of sins requires humbleness. You are acknowledging that you need a savior, a deliverer. You can move from hopelessness to hopefulness when you confess and repent of your sins. If you are real with yourself, you know your weakness, tendency, and soft spot.

Does this describe you? Are you hopeful and hopeless at the same time? Hopeful for change but doubtful that change will come to you. Of all the people at the pool, Jesus went to this man and offered him the very thing that he longed for. Jesus asked him if he wanted to be well. The man didn't respond to the question but rather explained why he would not be healed. Do you do the same thing? Jesus comes into your circumstance, and you tell Him why you will not be healed. Don't allow the enemy of your soul the entrance to keep reminding you of your failures. Acknowledge, repent, and move forward in God, and begin to live your best life.

Jesus is waiting for you to come in agreement with His Word. He is here to heal you. Answer the question, "Do you want to be made well"?

Prayer

Father, I acknowledge that I need You. I need You to make me whole. I've struggled to free myself from my iniquities, but I failed to come to You first. You said if I confess my weaknesses to You that You are faithful and just to forgive me and cleanse me. Forgive me, for I have sinned and fallen short of Your glory. You, oh Lord, created me in Your image and Your likeness. You are holy. Because You are holy, I can be holy too.

Your Word declares that the heart of man is desperately wicked. Father, create in me a clean heart and renew a right spirit within me. Cleanse my conscience from the memories of dead works. I lay aside the sin that has harassed me, now, Father, break its power over me so that I can walk in Your freedom. In Jesus' name, I pray. Amen.

Reflections

THE GLORY IN WAITING

Declaration

Father, I close the door that I propped open and let the enemy in to aggravate and annoy me. I choose to lay aside every weight and sin that has harassed and attacked me. I confessed my weaknesses to You. I declare that my body is the temple of the Holy Spirit, and You have free reign in my mind, my will, my emotions. I declare that I have come into agreement with Your Word concerning me. Now I am free to be victorious in every area of my life.

CHAPTER 4

My Soul is Waiting

⁵ I wait for the Lord, my soul waits, And in His word I do hope. 6 My soul waits for the Lord More than those who watch for the morning— Yes, more than those who watch for the morning.

PSALM 130:5-6 (NKJV)

Have you ever gone to the airport to pick someone up? You know their itinerary, and so you arrive early to the terminal to ensure that you don't miss them when they get off the plane. You may even be waiting with flowers, a sign, or balloons. You are anticipating their arrival. You are focused on the gate because you don't want to miss their entrance. Just like you are eagerly awaiting their arrival, in this passage, David is waiting and anticipating the presence of God.

David is saying, I look for hope and expect the Lord to show up in my situations and my circumstances. David's soul, his mind, will and emotions, everything within him, the very essence of who he is, waits, hopes, and expects the Lord. And because David knows God cannot lie, David relies on the Word of God. He trusts God because the Word of God caused him to have hope. Listen to Paul's words in Romans 5:1-5 (NKJV):

> Therefore, having been justified by faith, we have peace with God through our Lord Jesus Christ, [2] through whom also we have access by faith into this grace in which we stand, and rejoice in hope of the glory of God. [3] And not only *that*, but we also glory in tribulations, knowing that tribulation produces perseverance; [4] and perseverance, character; and character, hope. [5] Now hope does not disappoint, because the love of God has been poured out in our hearts by the Holy Spirit who was given to us.

Paul says that character produces hope, and hope does not disappoint or bring shame to us. Because God said it, David could hope for it. We can be like David and wait excitedly for Father God, knowing that He will not disappoint us. That is good news!

David didn't have a copy of the Bible from Genesis to Revelation, yet he trusted in the Word of the Lord. David in this Psalm is figuratively saying that he twists himself or plaits himself into God and then watches for the manifestation of the Word of God to come to pass in his life. Jesus is the Word made flesh, and He desires to be not just in our lives but a part of our lives down to the molecular level.

What are you waiting for? Do you have hope that is sustained in the Word of God? Can you say, "I hope in God because I have found Him to be trustworthy"? If you know that God doesn't lie, cannot fail, is all-seeing, all-knowing, all-powerful, then why doubt

Him? Why not take a few minutes to reflect on His faithfulness in your life. Even if you believe that life has dealt you a harsh hand, God has still been faithful to you.

Horatio Spafford is best known for the hymn, "It is Well with My Soul." His back story is that he and his wife were wealthy philanthropists and faithful members of the Lutheran church who made their home in Chicago. They had one son and four daughters. In 1871, their four-year-old son died from scarlet fever. A few short months later, the great Chicago fire destroyed most of their property holdings. Two years later, Horatio and Anna had planned a trip to sail to Europe with their daughters, but at the last minute, he had some business issues come up, and he was unable to go. He sent his wife and daughters ahead with plans to join them later. While his family was en route to Europe, another ship struck them, and their ship quickly sank.

The Spafford's lost their four daughters. His wife survived, and when she arrived in Wales, she sent her husband a telegram saying, "saved alone." Can you imagine the heartache and anguish of losing five children in less than three years? Would you blame them if they felt that God had forsaken them?

Maybe, your attitude would be like that of Job's wife when she urged Job to "curse God and die." Her sorrow at the loss of her children, their livelihood, Job's health had burdened her heart. Full of despair, she felt that the only way out of this pain was to curse God and die. In the middle of this calamity, the scriptures said Job worshipped. His response to his grief and his loss was worship.

If we're honest, many of us would not respond the same way. We may respond with anger or a decision to walk away from a relationship with God. We may respond with a religious front, but our hearts are far from believing and worshipping God. Job didn't see God as anything but God even in the midst of his worst nightmare.

Job said that the very thing he feared had come upon him. We do not know if his fear was of losing his children, his wealth, his health, a combination, or all the above, but we do know that tragedy had hit him hard. Like Job, Horatio had suffered a great loss. And like Job, he grieved, but more importantly, he worshipped.

When traveling to meet his wife, Anna, as the ship he was on neared the site of the misfortune that took his daughters, God inspired him to write the lyrics to one of the world's most beloved hymns. The hymn does not focus on his great loss but the faithfulness of God. He knew from experience that God is there and can comfort like none other, even during a season of overwhelming grief and sorrow.

In Psalm 42:5, David asks himself, "why are you cast down, O my soul?" Sometimes, we get depressed, stressed, battered, and bruised by life. Like David, you may have to ask yourself, why am I so down? Regardless of the reasons that come to mind as you answer your own question, know that you can trust God, hope in God, believe in God. You can have a blessed assurance that He has not forgotten about you, and He can and will give you the grace to not only get through but to come out victorious in any and all situations.

You should do the same as David, Job, and Horatio, and take inventory of your spiritual and mental state and then choose to trust and believe God to deliver you. David says that he will still praise God, who is the health of his countenance. God can turn the frown into a smile and take the sting out of horrible circumstances so that even the memories will point you to a loving and faithful God.

Depressed? Oppressed? Angry? Sad? Like a fisherman throwing a net into the water, cast your every care to Jesus, and He will heal your heart. Trust Him, and you, too, will be able to say, "It is well with my soul."

Prayer

Heavenly Father, thank You for Your loving care for me. Life has dealt me so many harsh blows, and I questioned why You allowed me to go through these situations. Father, I failed to realize that even when I was angry with You and not worshiping you in the process, Your grace and mercy were covering me. You pitied me, and although I felt like the pain would consume me, You didn't allow it. Thank you, Father. Like David, I want to excitedly wait for You to move in my life, in my home, in my relationships. Thank you that You grant new mercies every morning. I simply cannot deplete Heaven's storehouse of mercy.

Help me worship You in the process, as You heal my heart and memories. Help me, Father, persevere and develop character through the things I've suffered. Help me to trust You fully and completely. Help me to know You in the fellowship of Your sufferings. Help me, Lord, to be the best me, no longer broken, but whole, no longer angry but whole, no longer depressed but whole, no longer discontented but whole. I will be careful to give You the honor, the glory, and the praise, in Jesus' mighty name. Amen.

Reflections

THE GLORY IN WAITING

Declaration

I declare that I am an overcomer. I am more than a conqueror. No sorrow, depression, or anger will consume me and cause me not to worship my God. I am a worshipper in good times and in bad. I am consistent in my walk, knowing that I can trust You, Lord, to take care of all my needs.

I declare that I choose to wait with excitement and expectancy for God to come into my affairs and guide my footsteps into a victorious life. I declare that my trust is in the Lord, and in His Word, I will hope.

CHAPTER 5

They Are Laughing at Me

Through the Lord's mercies we are not consumed,
Because His compassions fail not.

LAMENTATIONS 3:22 (NKJV)

Have you ever felt that life had beaten you down? Sometimes, it seems like you can't catch a break. The air conditioner goes out in your car in the middle of summer, and the water heater blows up. You get the children's progress report only to find out there is not much to celebrate on that report. Your spouse falls ill, and the dog runs away. No matter how you look at your circumstances, you cannot see the silver lining for the black clouds.

On top of that, everybody seems to know your business. No matter where you go, you feel their eyes on you, and you hear the whispering as you walk by. It is enough to send you into a deep depression with no intentions of returning. Jeremiah describes it this way:

I have become the ridicule of all my people— Their taunting song all the day. He has filled me with bitterness, He has made me drink wormwood.

[16] He has also broken my teeth with gravel, And covered me with ashes. [17] You have moved my soul far from peace; I have forgotten prosperity. [18] And I said, "My strength and my hope have perished from the Lord." [19] Remember my affliction and roaming, The wormwood and the gall. [20] My soul still remembers And sinks within me. [21] This I recall to my mind, Therefore I have hope. [22] Through the Lord's mercies we are not consumed, Because His compassions fail not. Lamentations 3:14 -3:22 (NKJV)

Jeremiah reminds us that no matter what we go through, God is STILL good. Jeremiah recounted his afflictions, his wandering, his feeling alone and rejected. If he were alive today, he would say that his life had been put on blast. He was a laughingstock, and those around him would mock him and bully him. He was so depressed that he said he forgot what prosperity was. But he began to think about the goodness of God, and those thoughts changed his perspective. He said it is literally because of the Lord's mercies that we are not consumed. He declared great is the faithfulness of God. He then declares that the Lord is good to those who wait for Him, to the soul who seeks Him. It is good to wait on the Lord.

Life can come at you hard and knock the breath out of you. You may get up with skinned knees and bruises, wondering what just happened. Even amid hardships, Jeremiah tells us that we would have already been consumed if it weren't for the Lord's compassion.

THE GLORY IN WAITING

Waiting is hard to do when it is not done correctly. There is a right way and a wrong way to wait. People of purpose and destiny cannot develop the habit of killing time, of doing nothing while we wait on God. There is an old adage that says, "An idle mind is the devil's workshop." When your mind is idle, you become a target for the enemy to plant ungodly, unfaithful thoughts. Before you know it, you will be tempted, and like Eve, Satan will ask you the question, "Has God really said?" When your mind is idle and you have not been feeding on the Word of God, Satan will ask questions with the intent of causing you to doubt the Word of God.

David said in Psalm 119:11 that he had hidden the Word of God in his heart so that he would not sin against God. When you are waiting on God, reinforce the wait with the Word. You can hide or stockpile the Word through memorization. Memorizing scripture is an excellent tool to aid you in your growth and your walk with the Lord. There will be times when you will face temptation and not be able to get to your Bible or call your pastor. However, if you have hidden the Word in your heart, when you need to draw on that deposit, you will not experience insufficient funds or an overdraft.

In Matthew 25, Jesus shares the parable of the wise and the foolish virgins. It's a lesson on how to be prepared while waiting. The five wise took what they needed and extra, just in case, they had to wait longer than expected on the Lord. Whereas the five foolish took enough oil to get by, when the Lord delayed, they were not prepared. Only those who are prepared reap the benefits of the Lord's blessings. Preparation does not mean that you will not be tested.

David said, in Psalm 34:19, many are the afflictions of the righteous. Afflictions are the adversities you face, the calamities that occur in life, the sorrows you encounter. David says that the believer, the righteous, will face or have many afflictions, circumstances, and situations that will be negative, but there is good news. David goes on to say, "But the Lord delivers him out of them all." There is absolutely nothing that you will encounter that God cannot deliver you out of. Paul stated it this way in 1 Corinthians 10:13 (NKJV):

> No temptation has overtaken you except such as is common to man; but God is faithful, who will not allow you to be tempted beyond what you are able, but with the temptation will also make the way of escape, that you may be able to bear it.

God will not allow you to be tested, tried, tempted above your ability to handle it, but He will always give you a way of escape. In other words, if you are being tempted to sin, look for the escape. God has a way of escape for you. You need to look for it. It may be a door, a window, a tunnel, a hiding place, a cave, or behind a boulder. It is His responsibility to prepare the way of escape. It is your responsibility to look for it and use it. God's compassion is so great towards us; He will not fail us. He knows we could be consumed, but He doesn't allow it.

How are you preparing for the Lord in your life? When trials come, what do you do to stay true to purpose and on course with destiny? Do you allow what people are saying to distract you, to depress you? Do you allow your troubles to get you off focus? How are you plaiting your life to include Him?

THE GLORY IN WAITING

Prayer

Heavenly Father, sometimes the cares of life weigh me down, and I forget to release them back to You. I start out saying the right things, but as time goes on, I'm no longer talking and walking in faith. Forgive me, God, for not staying focused and not being prepared. Forgive me for not providing a place in my heart for Your Word to dwell and grow richly in me. Forgive me, Father, for allowing what others think of me to outweigh what You have said about me.

Father, I thank You for Your compassion towards me and Your loving kindness. You love me so much that You even prepare a way of escape when the enemy tempts me to disobey or not believe You. Father, I choose to trust You. I choose to believe Your Word. Help me to look for my escape route. May I love You more than any sin, any person, anything.

Thank you, Father God, for delivering me out of every affliction, every trial, and every test. Thank you for the ability to focus on You and Your Word. I have hidden Your Word in my heart that I will not sin against You. In Jesus' name, I pray. Amen.

Reflections

THE GLORY IN WAITING

Declaration

I declare that I am an overcomer through Him who loves me. I will not allow the enemy of my soul to taunt me about past mistakes. I will not put pleasing people above pleasing God. I will confess my faults to the Lord and allow Him to heal, deliver and set me free. I declare that no weapon formed against me shall prosper. I declare that no matter what comes my way, I stand on the fact that God is still good. God is my strong deliverer, and He is worth waiting for.

CHAPTER 6

Anointed Yet Waiting

But He knows the way that I take; When He has tested me, I shall come forth as gold.

JOB 23:10 (NKJV)

The Lord speaks a word over your life, and you are excited. The congregation claps; everyone agrees with you. After a while, that same word that brought you joy is now making you agitated. Why? Because you are in a holding pattern, you are waiting for the word to manifest.

What is a holding pattern? In aviation, a holding pattern is usually an oval course in the air in which planes circle the destination. The pilots are waiting for clearance from the air traffic controller to land the aircraft. Whenever it is deemed necessary, the air traffic controller places airplanes in a holding pattern to ensure the safety of those in the air and on the ground. The beauty of the holding pattern in your life is this, just because you are in a holding pattern doesn't mean you stop moving. Planes are not helicopters.

They are not designed to hover in one spot. They are designed for forward flight. Likewise, God has designed you for forward flight, even when you are waiting on Him to move, to give you clearance, you are not to become idle, you are to move in a controlled pattern, and in due season, he will give you clearance to land, blessing you and blessing others.

You can do nothing to make it come to pass, so you are looking at your watch and looking up into the heavens wondering when God is going to bring His Word to pass. You would not have even hoped for this, but God spoke the Word and said you would be king. Let's talk to David and see what he has to say. You know the story; David was out in the field taking care of his father's flocks. The prophet Samuel came to David's father, Jesse, and asked to see his sons. His father lined up seven of his sons and did not even think to send for the eighth son, for surely the Lord's anointed was in the older boys and not his youngest.

Depending on which scholar's estimation you adhere to, David was between 8 and 15 years old when he was anointed king. The Bible states that David was crowned king of Israel at age 30. At the very least, he had to wait 15 years between being anointed and seeing the manifestation of the declaration that he would be king. What did David do in the interim? He went back to the fields to tend his father's flocks. The problem with many of us is that we go sit down after God gives us a glimpse of our future. We wait by the door, doing nothing. If we look at David's example, he waited by serving. He went back to work. It was God's Word and, therefore, God's responsibility to bring it to pass. David's job was to keep on working until God made the change.

THE GLORY IN WAITING

In the meantime, he became proficient with a slingshot. He killed a bear and a lion that both tried to attack the sheep. In both instances, he faced bigger and stronger adversaries than he was trained to kill. Those battles, those experiences, prepared him to kill a giant. If he had been just sitting idly while watching the flocks, the bear and the lion could have killed several of the sheep, but instead, while waiting to be king, he honed his craft of warfare and drew closer to God through worship. The Bible said that David's heart captured God's attention. 1 Samuel 16:7 instructs us not to look at man's outward appearance but at a person's heart, just as God does.

David somehow managed to keep his mind free of the thoughts of the palace by remaining true to the very essence of his being. He worshipped God in the field while taking care of the sheep. He became acquainted with His voice. He learned strategy and strategic warfare, all while taking care of sheep. Fifteen years of development, fifteen years of serving his natural father without any acknowledgment that the word spoken over his life, the anointing as king, would come to pass.

David is a teenager when he is sent by his father to take provisions to his brothers who are fighting the Philistines. He hears Goliath taunting the armies of Israel, and a righteous indignation arises in him. His brothers discounted him because, after all, he was the last, the youngest. However, what they failed to see was that he was the anointed difference. What do I mean by anointed difference? He was the one handpicked by God for God to show His power through. He was the eighth son of Jesse, the new beginning.

Sometimes, those closest to us will not see the value or worth that God has placed in us and on us. Nevertheless, we must be like David and allow him to develop us in the field with our few sheep.

THE GLORY IN WAITING

We must master worshipping Father God when no one is around to applaud us. God can use us to His glory when we yield to the Spirit and allow Him to have full reign. David did not create the opportunity; God did. Let me say that again for the people in the back. David did not create, manipulate, or devise any plans to ascend to the throne. David worshipped God while he worked and waited for the Word spoken over his life to manifest.

God created an encounter that would bring glory to His name. Because David was an obedient vessel, God was able to take what David had perfected when no one was watching and put it on display for the world to see. In due season, David's devotion to God put him on the throne of Israel. All of this occurred because David learned how to worship and hear the voice of God while tending a few sheep in the field of his father.

What are you doing to bring God glory that no one sees? God knows the way that you will take on this journey called life. He knows the way, and He will test you, try you, and scrutinize you while you are in process. When you have passed the test, you will come out of it valuable as purified gold. God cannot use you if you have not been tested. David passed the test of worship and warfare while tending his father's sheep. When he was ready, God used him to shine for His glory.

Are you worshipping God through your service to others? David's ascent to the throne was not based on his being born into the right family. It was based on his heart posture to God. Take a moment right now and honestly reflect on your heart posture. If you are not where you should be, what can you do in private that will give God a reason to reward you openly in due season?

THE GLORY IN WAITING

Prayer

Dear Heavenly Father, the Bible says that You know the way that I will take. You know what decisions I will make in any given circumstance. Order my footsteps, oh Lord, so that I don't stray to the left nor the right but that I walk confidently in Your will. Father, I desire to fulfill the purpose for which You sent me to the earth to fulfill. Search my heart, oh Lord, and cleanse me from every evil scheme, thought process, every evil desire. Create in me a clean heart, oh God, and renew a right spirit within me. God, I want to be Your anointed difference, in my home, on my job, in my church, in my community.

As I wait on You, Father, may I be like David and develop my worship and spiritual warfare so that I will pass the test and avoid every temptation designed to bring me down when You bring me to the forefront. I thank you in advance for Your favor, in Jesus' name. Amen.

Reflections

THE GLORY IN WAITING

Declaration

I declare that I am a vessel of honor and God can trust me in private and in public arenas. I declare that I am the anointed difference for my home, job, church, and community. God designed me with purpose in mind, and I will complete the mission He sent me to fulfill.

CHAPTER 7

How Long, Lord?

For ye have need of patience, that, after ye have done the will of God, ye might receive the promise.

HEBREWS 10:36 (KJV)

In this passage of scripture, *hypomonē* is translated as patience. Patience is the ability to endure, to be constant, to be consistent. The person who is patient has the characteristic of an individual who is not moved from their purpose even when faced with trials or tribulations. Contrary to what some might believe, patience requires strength. It is not for the faint of heart. Patient people may bend, but they don't break. They have a "stick-to-it-ness." Patient people withstand the pressure in the process to obtain the prize at the end of the process. Patient people learn to stand in the midst of adversity. Even if what they are waiting on seems to be taking too long, they will wait.

It's easy to wait when you have no reason to be impatient. Let's look at David. He was the eighth son of Jesse, and the prophet

Samuel had anointed him to be the next king of Israel. David was God's choice.

David was not impatient with the prophetic word over his life because he was young and loved what he did. He loved taking care of the sheep. He loved worshipping His God. He loved spending time in nature. He was not impatient because his spiritual, emotional, and physical needs were being met.

Impatience rears its ugly head when we perceive or feel a deficit in our life. The deficit can be financial; it can be in our relationships or in our health. There may come a time when you find yourself like David in Psalm 13, crying out to God and asking him, "How long, Lord?".

> ¹How long, O LORD? Will You forget me forever? How long will You hide Your face from me? ²How long must I take counsel in my soul, *Having* sorrow in my heart day after day? How long will my enemy exalt himself *and* triumph over me? ³Consider and answer me, O LORD my God; Give light (life) to my eyes, or I will sleep the *sleep of* death,⁴ And my enemy will say, "I have overcome him," And my adversaries will rejoice when I am shaken. ⁵But I have trusted *and* relied on *and* been confident in Your lovingkindness *and* faithfulness; My heart shall rejoice *and* delight in Your salvation. ⁶I will sing to the LORD, Because He has dealt bountifully with me. Psalm 13 (AMP)

We do not know when David wrote this psalm, but we can surmise, this is not the teenaged David; this is the grown man. David going up against Goliath, expected God to move in that moment.

Here, David wanted to know how long before God avenged him of his enemies. He is questioning whether God has forgotten him. He is acknowledging God has not answered him immediately. This does not appear to be the first time he has prayed about this situation. He is mentally and emotionally drained. God is silent, and David is wondering when God will deliver him. Like David, you may be wondering about the journey you are on. You may find that you don't think like you used to.

Your perspective changes with living life. I've often heard older people tell those who are younger, "just keep living." In other words, if you haven't experienced hurt or betrayal or heartache and body aches, "just keep living." Some lessons you will only learn through experience and through time.

The young David did not shrink back from facing Goliath even when his older brothers tried to silence him and "shame" him into inaction. But in this psalm, David is focused on those who had lied on him, "hated" on him, mistreated, and misunderstood him, even tried to take his life. His focus is not on God but on what he has been through. David had become frustrated while waiting. If we are honest, frustration while waiting or are in the process is real.

Frustration is that feeling you get when you need something to change, but you don't have the ability to change it. Maybe you are struggling to reach a goal, such as weight loss or a production goal on your job, and no matter how hard you try, it feels as if you are spinning your wheels and going nowhere. You may become frustrated or vexed with people because of their personalities or their habits. Frustration may exhibit itself in your body by forming a knot in your stomach or tension in your shoulders. Maybe it shows up as a migraine, overeating, anorexia, alcohol abuse, or biting your nails.

However, frustration manifests in your life. Know that God does not have you waiting to annoy and irritate you. In Galatians 6:9 (NKJV), Paul encouraged the believers at Galatia with these words: "And let us not grow weary while doing good, for in due season we shall reap if we do not lose heart." The Message Bible states it this way: "So let's not allow ourselves to get fatigued doing good. At the right time we will harvest a good crop if we don't give up or quit." In other words, you have planted your seeds in good ground. Just because you don't see the produce yet doesn't mean that change is not occurring under the soil. You will have a good crop in the appropriate season. Just don't quit, don't give up!

If you are doing all you know how to do, trust God in the process and the outcome. God is not sadistic and cruel, taking pleasure in your irritation. It does not give God joy to see you frustrated. The Bible says that David was a man after God's own heart, and yet, in this psalm, we see that David was frustrated, irked, agitated, aggravated, defeated, perplexed, anxious.

Yes, we can relate to David. Like him, we, too, have asked God when we would be vindicated. We, too, have taken our eyes off God and placed them on the circumstance. But we don't have to stay off focus. Just like David, we may start off complaining (verses 1-2), but as he did, we will move to pray (verses 3-4), and through prayer, we will move back into faith, into trusting and believing God because we will remember that God has been good to us. We know that since He cannot lie and cannot change, we can trust that He will show His goodness to us again.

Imagine an athlete running a marathon, he has a good pace, but he has become irritated because he can't seem to separate himself from the two runners who are nipping at his feet. He's tired of the agitation that he feels. Rather than allowing the other runners to motivate him to be a better runner, to be more strategic, he allows them to get in his head, and it causes frustration. He becomes so frustrated that he lets up and just stops running. What he didn't realize was that he was close to victory. If he had just pressed through his frustration, he would have won the race. The runners on either side of him were disqualified, and the others were too far behind. But he was tired of fighting for what he felt should have come easier to him. He eventually convinced himself that he wouldn't win, and he gave up; he quit. He didn't win the race because he stopped running. It had nothing to do with the other runners; the issue was within himself.

Take a moment to reflect. What situations in life took you off focus? What problems, what relationships caused you to doubt God? What relationship, whether personal or business, made you want to throw in the towel? Why did you stop running?

Did you allow frustration and impatience to take you out of the game? Did you feel abandoned, dejected, rejected? If so, consider how you can get back in the race. Maybe you feel that God is testing you because He isn't answering your questions. Remember that the teacher is silent when administering the test. The writer of Hebrews lets us know that we receive the promise through endurance. Rest if you must but stay in the race. You will obtain the promise if you don't quit. Remember the adage: "A quitter never wins, and a winner never quits."

Prayer

Dear Heavenly Father,

THE GLORY IN WAITING

Sometimes I get so frustrated with where I am in life. I feel like a failure or that I have failed You. I look at others around me, and they seem to be progressing while I am standing still. Help me, oh God, to get my focus back on You. I realize that the frustration comes when my life is out of balance. Help me to balance spending time with You, taking care of my family, doing my job, taking care of me. Sometimes my to-do list is so long, and I'm waiting for help that seems as if it will never arrive. Help me to stop focusing on what's wrong and to begin to focus on YOU. I will keep my eyes on You, and I will not give up, give in, or give out.

Thank you for changing my heart and my thought process. I can do all things through Christ. You are faithful. And because You are faithful, I know that you will reward me as I stay true to my purpose. Thank you. In Jesus' name, I pray. Amen.

Reflections

THE GLORY IN WAITING

Declaration

I declare that I have sown in faith and because I have sown in faith, I declare that I will reap a bountiful harvest. I will focus on Jesus, who is the author and the finisher of my faith. I will not give in, give out, or give up, but I will have the courage and the patience to endure to the end. I am more than a conqueror through Jesus Christ, and it is because of Him, I have the victory!

CHAPTER 8

Transformed Service

But be transformed by the renewing of your mind...

ROMANS 12:2B (NKJV).

Have you ever been to a restaurant and been served by someone who is in training? I have, and the experience each time has been quite pleasant. Why would being served by a trainee be pleasant? My guess is that when in training, the server is paying attention to the instructions given and are careful to do as instructed because the teacher is observing. Sometimes, the trainee observes while the trainer serves. Other times the trainee serves while the trainer watches. In these instances, the goal is twofold: training and service. The hope is to train the individual to wait on customers according to their business model. Secondly, the quality of service should not be diminished due to the training.

In the natural, what are the characteristics of a good server/waiter?

THE GLORY IN WAITING

Characteristic	Description
Friendly	Greet customers with a smile.
Attentive	Observant, focused, passionate about providing good service.
Knowledgeable of the menu	Able to assist the customer in menu choices.
Timely	Timely in greeting, seating, order taking, serving meals, and bringing the check.
Dress	Uniform is clean, wrinkle-free, and the server is well-groomed with clean nails.

Good customer service encompasses all of these at the very minimum. Conversely, there have been other times that I have gone to a restaurant and received poor, rude, or non-existent service. Whether a five-star restaurant or your favorite fast-food restaurant, the service should be good.

In the natural, what are some of the characteristics of a bad server/waiter?

Characteristic	Description
Unfriendly	Greeting to customers is not warm or inviting.

Inattentive	Not observant, unorganized, unfocused, impatient.
Unknowledgeable	Unable and/or unwilling to assist in menu choices.
Untimely	Must be summoned for everything, even a glass of water. Server is "ghost."
Dress	Uniform is stained, or the server appears disheveled.

In both cases you had a server, but the type of server, the characteristics of the server, determined the quality of the service. Good service will often override food that is not tasty or of poor quality. In other words, the overall experience was positive not because of the food but because of the service received.

The same can be said about Christians. Christians should be exhibiting Christ-like behavior, but sadly, the inconsistency that many believers display in their daily lives will have those encountering them asking to speak to management because they know that they are not reflecting His business model. In Matthew 21:12-17, Jesus was so upset that the Father's business model was not being followed that he drove out all who were engaging in commerce in the temple. He then modeled what should be the standard in the temple: healing the blind and the lame. Are you following Jesus' example? Listen to what Jesus said:

> If anyone serves Me, he must [continue to faithfully] follow Me [without hesitation, holding steadfastly to

Me, conforming to My example in living and, if need be, suffering or perhaps dying because of faith in Me]; and wherever I am [in heaven's glory], there will My servant be also. If anyone serves Me, the Father will honor him.

John 12: 26 (AMP)

Deciding to follow Jesus is not just a song to sing at Bible camp. Jesus said those who follow Him must conform to His example in living, and, if need be, suffering. When we serve others, we should do so in a manner that brings glory to Jesus, not to ourselves. We are not our own; we represent Jesus. We represent the kingdom of God in the earth realm. As His representatives, we must exhibit Christ-like characteristics, or else we are not honoring Him.

How then can we honor Christ? How can a server move from mediocrity to excellence? Application of the truths of the Word of God. 2 Corinthians 5:17 (KJV) states: "Therefore if any man be in Christ, he is a new creature: old things are passed away; behold, all things are become new." Christ in the life of a believer can transform you from mediocrity. If you are in Christ, "in" suggests a fixed position or within a place, time, or state. Thus, I would venture to say, if any man is plaited in Christ, he is a new creature. That man has been transformed. The transformation of a waiter comes from within. You must allow God to transform you from someone who is impatiently serving to someone who is passionately serving.

Paul, in his epistle to the Romans, wrote in the 12th chapter, verses 1-2 (NKJV)

I beseech you therefore, brethren, by the mercies of God, that you present your bodies a living sacrifice, holy, acceptable to God, which is your reasonable service. 2 And do not be conformed to this world, but be transformed by the renewing of your mind, that you may prove what is that good and acceptable and perfect will of God.

In the Greek, the word *conform* means to fashion one's mind and character to another's. Conformation, in this sense, is an external action. Paul is saying, do not fashion or make yourself, nor do you allow others to press you into a mold! The change cannot come from your works. You must be transformed. You must go through a "metamorphose." We are familiar with that word because of the changes that a caterpillar goes through to become a butterfly. The change occurs from the inside, and when it is complete, it manifests on the outside. True change occurs from within. The psalmist said, in Psalm 139:13-16 (NKJV):

> For You formed my inward parts; You covered me in my mother's womb. [14] I will praise You, for I am fearfully and wonderfully made; Marvelous are Your works, And that my soul knows very well. [15] My frame was not hidden from You, When I was made in secret, And skillfully wrought in the lowest parts of the earth. [16] Your eyes saw my substance, being yet unformed.

The change isn't even visible until it is completed. The caterpillar weaves a cocoon, and from the outside, it does not appear that anything is happening, but, on the inside, a change is taking place. No longer relegated to just crawling on leaves, the caterpillar emerges as a beautiful butterfly able to fly when the change is complete. Ultimately, transformation is a work of the Spirit. He works on your heart, on your mind, helps balance your emotions, convicts you of sin and sinful thoughts. He enables you or gives you the strength to go through the spiritual process of pruning, removing dead issues from your life so that new life can be experienced. Indeed, the change doesn't take place in the public; it takes place in the innermost parts.

Do you need a transformation? Does your attitude need an adjustment? Do you reflect Christ in your home, on your job, when you are in the store, at a game, in a restaurant? What change needs to take place in you that only the Holy Spirit can work?

Prayer

Dear Heavenly Father,

I have not always represented You as I should. Sometimes my attitude was wrong. Other times, I was serving, but it was not with a spirit of excellence. I was preoccupied with the cares of life. Forgive me, Lord. Help me not to be impatient when serving others. I choose to be passionate about my walk, my lifestyle, and my ministry. Change my heart, oh God, and make it new. I acknowledge that You are the potter, and I am the clay. Please mold me into a vessel fit for Your use. I desire to be used by You. Thank you for the opportunity to serve You. I am humbled and honored. As I wait on You, teach me how to wait on others. In Jesus' name, I pray. Amen.

Reflections

THE GLORY IN WAITING

_____

_____

_____

_____

_____

_____

_____

_____

_____

_____

_____

_____

_____

_____

_____

_____

_____

_____

_____

_____

Declaration

I declare that I will renew my mind daily by spending time in the Word and in prayer. I declare that I will develop and operate in a spirit of excellence in all things. I will not resist the work of the Holy Spirit in my heart. I can do all things through Christ. I choose to serve God and to serve others with a passion that comes from God. I will not misrepresent God in my service. My love for God will be reflected in my love and care for others.

CHAPTER 9

The Place of Change

But as for you, you meant evil against me; but God
meant it for good...

GENESIS 50:20A (NKJV)

Have you ever felt that life was unfair, that you did not deserve the experiences, the circumstances you found yourself in? Maybe you were abused, raped, falsely accused of stealing, taunted because of your skin color, hair, eyes, body shape, or bullied by someone more popular or physically stronger than you. Maybe you were poor, or it could be you were rich, possibly you were conceived out of wedlock or due to incest or an affair. Perhaps your supervisor disliked you, and he or she made your workdays difficult. No matter the situation, waiting on God will produce victory in your life. Let's look at Joseph's story in Genesis chapters 37, 39-41.

Joseph was his father's favorite son, and his ten older brothers knew it. "Now Israel loved Joseph more than all his children, because he was the son of his old age. Also he made him a tunic of many colors" Genesis 37:3 (NKJV). Although he was his father's favorite child, he longed for his brothers' acceptance. There is no way Joseph thought that his brothers would betray him and plot to kill him. Imagine the emotions he had to deal with as a teen, alone and now betrayed and sold by his brothers into slavery.

Placed in a pit, he was rescued from the pit only to be sold into slavery to Egyptians. He was sold to the captain of the guard, who was one of Pharaoh's high-ranking officials named Potiphar. Think about it. Joseph was not accustomed to hard work. He was spoiled, and because his father favored him, he probably did not require Joseph to perform the same chores and tasks as his older brothers. Since Joseph was now a slave, he had to learn to work and to do so quickly. Even though he lacked real life experience with hard work, we see that Joseph served Potiphar with an excellent spirit.

God endowed Joseph with the gifts of management and administration. Along with his work ethic, these giftings earned him a position of trust in Potiphar's house. The only thing off-limits to Joseph in Potiphar's house was Potiphar's wife. He was grateful for the favor of Potiphar and was loyal to him

However, Potiphar wasn't the only one who saw Joseph's characteristics. The Bible says that Joseph was very handsome, and Potiphar's wife took notice. Potiphar's wife desired Joseph and tried to get him to lay with her on several occasions. He refused because he was a man of integrity and trustworthiness. When she failed to get him to do as she desired, she accused him of attempted rape.

When Potiphar's wife lied to him and told him that Joseph attempted to rape her, the Bible says that Potiphar's wrath was kindled. In this passage, the word translated wrath in this passage, aph, literally means nostrils flaring or snorting. Potiphar was enraged. At that moment, he could have killed Joseph or ordered that he be killed. Instead, he had Joseph placed in prison.

Once again, Joseph is bound in a situation that would significantly alter his life through no fault or malice of his own. While he is in prison, we see his maturation and the further development of his character. He was first betrayed by his brothers and now by Potiphar's wife. He had every reason to be bitter, to feel sorry for himself. Yet, somehow, these experiences drew him closer to Father God. Joseph's change took place in a prison, a place that he did not "earn." It was not his sin that put him in prison; it was his integrity. He was charged with attempted rape. Why was his life spared? Let's look for a moment at Potiphar.

Potiphar was the captain of the guard for Pharaoh. Killing Joseph would not have been out of his character. Potiphar's name means bull of Africa, a fat bull. Bulls are known for their anger. Potiphar could have had the mindset that Joseph was an ungrateful servant and deserved death for attempting to defile his wife.

Is it possible that Potiphar did not fully believe that Joseph had attempted to rape his wife? Is it possible that he looked at the evidence, Joseph's clothes in her hand, and wondered why his wife's clothes were not torn since allegedly Joseph attempted to have his way with her? If so, rather than embarrass his wife or bring shame or dishonor to himself, he had Joseph jailed rather than executed. Potiphar's duties may have included oversight of the warden of the prison. Is it possible that Joseph's integrity in serving Potiphar caused Potiphar to spare his life and to recommend him to the warden?

God had a purpose for Joseph that was established before he was born. Joseph would be used to preserve the nation of Israel. His brothers did not know it, his parents did not know it, but God intentionally created Joseph for that time. The prophet Jeremiah wrote in Jeremiah 29:11 (NKJV), "For I know the thoughts that I think toward you, says the Lord, thoughts of peace and not of evil, to give you a future and a hope." God created each of us with purpose and sent us into the earth realm when He needed us to appear on the scene. Even when it looks like all hell is fighting against us and winning, God can turn everything around for our good. When we submit to His lordship, we discover that "all things work together for good to those who love God, to those who are the called according to His purpose" (Romans 8:28 NKJV). God works on the situation, and He works on us.

Transformation will not always be visible to the public eye, but when transformation has taken place, the public will see the final result. Film is developed in the dark, babies are developed in the womb, seeds are developed in the earth. True growth occurs in the secret place. Do you want to be transformed? Stop trying to make the changes for others to see and allow God to work on the innermost part of you. Allow Him to develop your character.

The Lord chastens those that He loves. Allow Him to correct you. The Bible says in 2 Timothy 3:16-17 that all scripture is given by inspiration from God. In other words, all scripture is God-breathed and is profitable for doctrine, for reproof, for correction. If God cannot correct you, then you are not his child. God will use people to be sandpaper in your life to agitate and aggravate you in order to smooth out your rough edges.

THE GLORY IN WAITING

Joseph may have wondered for several years how things would work out where he would be in charge. Joseph probably stopped trying to see how the dreams from his youth would be fulfilled. How would his family "bow" to him when they are in Canaan, and he is in Egypt? Maybe he thought that he would ascend to power from Potiphar's house. However, Potiphar's house led to the prison. Surely just through self-preservation alone, Joseph could no longer focus on the dream from so many years before; he was now only focused on his relationship with the Lord.

Joseph was a lad, a teen when he was first given the dream about the stars bowing down. He was 17 years old when he was sold as a slave by his brothers. He spent approximately 11 years combined in Potiphar's house and in prison. While in prison, he was 28 years old when he interpreted the dreams for the butler and the baker.

In Genesis 41:46, the scripture says that Joseph was 30 years old when he entered Pharaoh's service. By the time Pharaoh needed his dream interpreted, Joseph was no longer looking to men to advocate for him but to God. Because he was now wholly disciplined in his emotions and thought process, the wait for the fulfillment of his dream was no longer an issue.

During the "wait" between the dream and fulfilling the dream, God did his work in Joseph. Even though life had been unfair, filled with jealousy, betrayal, resentment, displacement, and abandonment, he did not let the experiences make him bitter; they made him better. God predestined Joseph to be a savior, a deliverer of the Israelites. Joseph was strategically placed in Egypt to preserve the Messianic line. What the devil meant for evil, God worked for Joseph's good.

Joseph was transformed from a spoiled child to a mature leader, a loving son, and a forgiving brother. All of this happened while he was in slavery and in prison. With everything that had transpired in his life, the betrayals, the abandonment, and rejection, Joseph learned forgiveness. He believed in forgiveness so much that he named one of his sons, Manasseh, "causing to forget." In other words, God had caused him to forget the pain of betrayal, abandonment, and rejection. Instead of those negative emotions eating away at him, Joseph allowed God to heal his heart and fill it with love, compassion, and forgiveness.

Think of your life's experiences. When did you do your greatest learning? Were your greatest life's lessons learned in the public eye or when you were obscure? When did your greatest character development take place?

Prayer

Dear Heavenly Father,

Your Word declares that you order the footsteps of the righteous. I realize that my disobedience and some of my decisions have caused detours in my life. But You, Father, have always been faithful to guide me back onto the path that You laid out for me. Father, You even took my mistakes and missteps and worked them for my good. I'm grateful that in spite of me, You still are guiding me into purpose. Thank you, Father. Your Word is sure. You who have begun the good work in me, YOU are faithful, and for that, I am thankful. In response, Father, I willingly lay down my perceptions of how You will work Your will in me. I humbly submit and yield to Your direction and management of my life. In Jesus' name, I pray. Amen.

Reflections

THE GLORY IN WAITING

Declaration

I declare that I am a person of integrity. I will represent God well, no matter the circumstance I find myself in. I choose to forgive those who have intentionally hurt me. I will not allow bitterness or anger to block me from progressing and growing in God. I declare that I am the righteousness of God in Christ Jesus and that because of Him, I can do greater works in Jesus' name.

CHAPTER 10

Waiting for the Promise

Is anything too hard for the Lord?

GENESIS 18:14A (NKJV)

There are seven women in the Bible that are described as barren. We will briefly discuss three: Hannah, wife of Elkanah (1 Samuel 1:5-11), Sarah, wife of Abraham (Genesis 18:10-14), and Rebekah, wife of Isaac (Genesis 25:21-23).

In 1st Samuel, chapter 1, we are introduced to Elkanah, Hannah, and Peninnah. Elkanah was a wealthy man, and he had two wives: Hannah and Peninnah. Hannah was the wife he loved and favored. He openly expressed his love for her by the gifts he showered on her. Peninnah was his second wife. She bore him ten sons and two daughters, all before Hannah had her first child.

Culturally, if a man was married for ten years and he and his wife had no children, he was to take a second wife so that he could be in obedience to the edict given Adam and Eve in the garden, "to be fruitful and multiply." Often, the wife would suggest to the husband that he should take a second wife, such as we'll see in the story of Abraham, Sarah, and Hagar.

According to Jewish tradition, Hannah had been barren for at least 19 years. She was a righteous woman, and yet she suffered from barrenness. In fact, the Bible says that the Lord closed her womb as if He closed a door. Hannah was barren, and it was the Lord's doing.

Have you ever been unproductive, and yet it was God that caused you to be unproductive? Everyone around you is producing with ease. You should be able to match their production, but all you seem to be able to do is watch. If God is causing your barrenness, trust the Lord, it is a setup. Know that if He closed the door, He is able to open the door.

Although little of the interaction between Hannah and Peninnah is in the Bible, what we do see is that Peninnah taunted and teased Hannah about her barrenness. Possibly, Peninnah was jealous of Elkanah's love and affection for Hannah and felt that Elkanah should have divorced Hannah or at least "demoted" her because of her barrenness. Perhaps, Peninnah thought that because she had borne him 12 children, Elkanah should love her more. Regardless of her reasoning for taunting Hannah, we see that the taunting and the bullying of Hannah drove Hannah into the presence of God. What the enemy meant for evil, God used it for Hannah's good. If Peninnah had realized that her jealousy and her taunting of Hannah would drive her into the presence of God, where she would obtain His favor, I'm sure she would not have done it.

Despite things not going her way, Hannah remained humble and graceful. Her character, her demeanor, was such that her husband doted on her and attempted to spoil her. Elkanah tried his best to let Hannah know that she did not have to give him children in order for him to love her. He asked Hannah, "Aren't I better to you than ten sons?" Elkanah fathered ten sons with Peninnah, yet he loved Hannah so much that he would give her a double portion. Elkanah saw the inward beauty of his wife's spirit and sought to ease her emotional anguish. The ache in Hannah's soul could not be fixed with gifts from her husband. Hannah needed a healing that only God could provide.

Hannah brought her complaint to the Lord. She did not lash out at Peninnah. She did not lash out at her husband. She took her complaint to the Lord. Nineteen years of barrenness. Nine years or more of bullying. Hannah was tired, frustrated, and hurt, but Hannah was wise. She went to the one that could answer her prayer and deliver her soul.

Hannah trusted that the Lord would answer her prayer. We see her pour out her heart to the Lord, empty herself of bitterness, of sorrow. She did so with so much fervor that Eli, the high priest, thought she was drunk. Hannah prayed a prayer that we can model because her prayer is the kind of prayer that God answers. There is an old hymn that says, "take your burdens to the Lord and leave them there." Her barrenness had become too much for Hannah to bear, so she prayed. In her prayer, Hannah told God that if He blessed her with a son, she would dedicate that child back to Him.

In Hebrews chapter 11, Sarah is listed in the "Faith Hall of Fame." How did she manage that? Surely, she never doubted God. She was a woman of faith, right? In Genesis 18:9-14 (NKJV), we see that Sarah had given up on the promise that God made to Abraham that she and Abraham would have a son.

9 Then they said to him, "Where *is* Sarah your wife?"

So he said, "Here, in the tent." 10 And He said, "I will certainly return to you according to the time of life, and behold, Sarah your wife shall have a son." (Sarah was listening in the tent door which *was* behind him.) 11 Now Abraham and Sarah were old, well advanced in age; *and*]Sarah had passed the age of childbearing. 12 Therefore Sarah laughed within herself, saying, "After I have grown old, shall I have pleasure, my lord being old also?" 13 And the LORD said to Abraham, "Why did Sarah laugh, saying, 'Shall I surely bear *a child,* since I am old?' 14 Is anything too hard for the LORD? At the appointed time I will return to you, according to the time of life, and Sarah shall have a son."

Sarah laughed because she forgot that Father God closed the door to her womb, so He had the key to unlock and open the door and produce the miracle that the open door required. Like Sarah, we get amnesia. We forget that God can do anything but fail. If He said it, He could bring it to pass. Do you see the testimony? What is a greater testimony in your life than one of resurrection? Your marriage is dead. Your business is dead. Your health is failing. If possible, in your own strength, you would have ensured that your spouse did not walk away, your business was a household brand, and your health was perfect. Would God have gotten the glory for those accomplishments, or would you? However, when everyone can see that you cannot work the miracle you need, God's Word can still perform. His Word will not return to Him void, but it will accomplish what He sent it to do. So, laugh if you want to, but God has the last laugh, just ask Sarah.

Rebekah was the daughter-in-law of Abraham and Sarah. Like Sarah, she, too, experienced barrenness. Although cultural tradition said Isaac should take a second wife after ten years, Isaac did not. He loved Rebekah, and she loved him. They both prayed fervently that God would open her womb. Maybe Isaac's experience with his older brother, Ishmael, caused them to say, we'll wait.

Ishmael was the son born of the union between Hagar and Abraham after Sarah's desperation to have a child drove her to encourage her husband to sleep with another woman. Honestly, most of us today cannot wrap our brains around that scenario. However, it is easy to judge them from our vantage point. What Sarah did would be the modern-day surrogacy option. Ishmael had Abraham's DNA. Ishmael was produced out of impatience, out of a desire more for the child than for the giver of the child. Sarah and Hannah had to deal with the repercussions of doing things the way that society dictated.

In Sarah's case, we know that God said that she and Abraham would have a child. Sarah was already old when the word was spoken, but there was still a chance for that "menopausal" surprise baby. But because Sarah (and society) viewed time as her enemy, she redefined the Word of the Lord to include giving her handmaiden, Hagar, to her husband. The unintended result was the emotional baggage that Ishmael had. The scriptures state that when Sarah saw Ishmael mocking Isaac, she told Abraham to kick them out.

Ishmael was a teenager when Isaac was born. For years, his father had doted on him and him only. Now, this baby had "stolen" his father's attention. I believe it was somewhat natural for Ishmael to resent Isaac. Ishmael's mother was not a wife, just a concubine. She had even fewer rights. No doubt Ishmael saw how his mother was being treated, and as a child, he was limited in his ability to do anything about his mother's status. This promised child, Isaac, his little brother, was a gamechanger, and Ishmael didn't like it.

God fulfilled his promise to Sarah and Abraham and gave them a son, but the child created out of impatience provided unintended challenges and issues. Think over your life and your decisions when you were impatient with God. Since God is able to work all things for our good, He turns our mess into a message. He delivers us out of the stench of sinful pride and hidden shame. Pride and shame are two sides of the same coin, and neither brings glory to God. We feel the need to assist God in bringing His Word to pass so we move in our own strength. Moving in our own strength will cause us to sometimes veer off the path that God has created for us.

Often, when the weight of life gets too heavy for us, we drink, use drugs, illicit sex, become tv addicts, overeat, become fitness fanatics, withdraw, etc. We find ways to appease our feelings without releasing our souls from anguish. If not properly dealt with, the weight manifests itself in destructive mindsets and destructive behavior. Proverbs 23:7 says, "as a man thinks in his heart so is he."

What are you thinking? How are you processing the wait? Are you going to Father God with a pure heart? If not, are you going to Him to purify your heart? Are you praying with purpose, or are you increasingly religious? You have the systems of religion but no relationship with God. You go to church, Bible Study, prayer meeting, missionary society, evangelism outreach, sing in the choir, usher, serve on the administration team, but your heart is far from it because God disappointed you by making you wait for deliverance.

Why would He make you wait? Why is your neighbor able to have children like she's a rabbit and you can't even give birth to one? Why are your co-workers promoted when everyone knows that their attitudes are awful or that they don't possess the knowledge or experience you do? Why were you passed over? Is it possible that God is waiting on you and wants to use you for His glory? The writer of Hebrews in chapter 12 verse 1 implores us to lay aside every weight and the sin which does so easily beset us and let us run with patience the race that is set before us.

Sarah was impatient, and for a little while, she operated in unbelief. She did not trust that God would give her a son. On the other hand, Rebekah did not ask Isaac to go outside of their marriage to produce a child. She waited, and God blessed her with twins. Rebekah's error came when she "assisted" God in bringing His Word to pass regarding Jacob ruling over Esau. Esau was the eldest son, but Jacob was the child through which the covenant blessing would flow. Rebekah's natural mind did not understand how God would do that. Her manipulative actions and influence caused Jacob to literally have to run for his life. By favoring Jacob over Esau and influencing him to steal Esau's blessing, she created a situation in which Esau wanted to kill his brother and had decided he would do so after their father had passed. It would be years before the "assistance" of Rebekah was rooted out of the brother's relationship, thereby allowing them to be in the right relationship with each other.

Hannah waited on God to change her situation. But she also let God know that if He blessed her with what she asked of Him, she would dedicate that child to Him. In other words, she told God that

He was more important to her than the desire to have the child. Wow! You are barren; you want a child. The only one who can give you a child is Father God because He is the only one who can "open the door" that He closed. Like Hannah, we can cry out to God and trust that He hears us and that He is ready and able to answer our prayers and open the door to the blessing that we are seeking.

Prayer

Dear Heavenly Father,

I come to You realizing that I have some areas of unfruitfulness and barrenness. I have been impatient in the process and have said or done things in unbelief because I did not see You moving. Father, I repent for my impatience. When Your promises seemed afar off, I took matters into my own hands. My actions resulted in me straying from Your presence. Oh Father, please forgive me and create in me a clean heart and renew a right spirit within me.

Father, unlock the doors of fruitfulness in my life so that I may serve You in purpose. Cause me to see time as a tool and not as an enemy. May I use time wisely and trust that You are able to step into time, into my situation, and make all things right. May I learn to trust You and run to You, knowing that You are able to open my natural womb and my spiritual womb and cause me to produce life. Thank you, Lord, for fruitfulness. In Jesus' name. Amen.

Reflections

THE GLORY IN WAITING

Declaration

I declare that I am no longer barren, but I am fruitful. God has opened my womb to receive His purpose. I walk in divine wholeness: physically, spiritually, and emotionally. I refuse to be impatient because I know that He who has begun a new work in me is faithful to complete it.

CHAPTER 11

No Assistance Needed

So shall My word be that goes forth from My mouth; It shall not return to Me void, But it shall accomplish what I please, And it shall prosper in the thing for which I sent it.

ISAIAH 55:11 (NKJV)

Sometimes we mean well, but we do the wrong thing for the right reason. God says you will be great; your seed will be like the sand on the seashore. Great word, but when it doesn't happen when you think it should, you've got to do something, right? So rather than wait on God to perform His Word, you resort to cultural traditions or, even worse, character flaws to accomplish His will. God doesn't need that kind of help. Let's look at Jacob.

In the 25th chapter of Genesis, Rebekah is married to Isaac, but she is barren. Isaac prays for his wife to conceive, and God opens her womb. She is extremely uncomfortable during her pregnancy, and she prays and asks God why she is in so much discomfort. God speaks to Rebekah and lets her know she is carrying twins.

> [21] Isaac prayed to the Lord for his wife, because she was unable to conceive children; and the Lord granted his prayer and Rebekah his wife conceived [twins]. [22] But the children struggled together within her [kicking and shoving one another]; and she said, "If it is so [that the Lord has heard our prayer], why then am I this way?" So she went to inquire of the Lord [praying for an answer]. [23] The Lord said to her, "[The founders of] two nations are in your womb; And the separation of two nations has begun in your body; The one people shall be stronger than the other; And the older shall serve the younger."
> Genesis 25: 21-23 (AMP)

God had indeed answered her husband's prayer, opened her womb, and was now blessing her with not one but two babies. But notice, God also gave her insight into the destinies of the twins. She gave birth to Esau and Jacob, and the struggle she felt in the womb began to play out in the natural.

Culturally, firstborn sons receive the birthright (double portion from their father) as well as a blessing. Esau was the firstborn, but the promise according to God's Word was on Jacob. Maybe for that reason, she favored Jacob. We cannot speculate because the text does not give us that insight into Rebekah.

The twins grow into men with different passions and purposes in life. Esau was an outdoorsman; he was skilled in hunting, and he loved it. Jacob was more of a mama's boy and stayed around his mother in the tent. In the 27th chapter, Jacob deceives Esau and takes Esau's birthright. While Esau should have valued his birthright, Jacob should not have used trickery to get his brother's birthright. Esau knows that he still has his father's blessing and takes comfort in that.

Fast forward, years later, Isaac is nearing death. He knows it, and so does his family. Rebekah overhears her husband instruct Esau to go and hunt game, prepare it, and serve it to him, and he will pronounce the blessing over him. Esau does as he is instructed. Isaac was about to bless Esau and Rebekah, remembering what God spoke to her before her children were born, thought within herself that she had to do something. She felt that she had to assist God in bringing His prophetic word to pass.

Jacob was 77 years old when Rebekah instructed, aided, and abetted Jacob into deceiving Isaac, who was 137 years old. Surely, if the Word of the Lord was coming to pass, He needed their assistance. Rebekah held dear in her heart the word that God had spoken to her about her sons. Meanwhile, Jacob does as his mother instructs and deceives his father into thinking he is Esau so that he can receive the blessing. Jacob is successful in his deception, and his father gives him the blessing that should have gone to Esau.

Jacob had obtained the birthright and the blessing that rightfully belonged to his brother through trickery and deception. When Esau comes before his father to be blessed, he discovers that his brother had outwitted him again. This time, Esau's wrath would not be easily appeased, and he determined that after he buried their father, he would kill his brother for all of the deceit and the thievery. Seeing how enraged Esau had become, Rebekah must now send her favorite son away to save his life. Both she and her husband will die without seeing Jacob alive again. Likewise, Jacob will not see his beloved parents again and has to literally run for his life and start a new life elsewhere.

All of this occurred because he and his mother decided to help God bring his Word to pass. Rebekah remembered what He said; she just forgot that He was able to bring it to pass. God does not need to use a device of Satan (lying, deceit, trickery) to bring His will to pass. God can righteously fulfill His Word.

How many times has God promised you or showed you something, and then you decided to take matters into your own hands to help God out because He clearly was oblivious to time? God had shown Rebekah that Jacob would rule over his brother. Undoubtedly, she groomed him as he cooperated without much resistance to her scheme. Jacob wanted the blessing that belonged to his brother. Rebekah loved both of her sons, but possibly Jacob became her favorite son because God showed her a glimpse of his destiny.

Jacob runs to his uncle, Rebekah's brother, Laban. He will soon find out that Laban is a better trickster than he is. Jacob meets Rachel and falls in love with her. He agrees to work seven years for Laban, after which he can marry Rachel. On the wedding night, Laban tricks Jacob, and instead of marrying Rachel, he is married to Leah. Laban didn't honor his word, but if Jacob wanted Rachel, he would have to make another contract with Laban. Jacob agrees to work another seven years for Rachel. The trickster was tricked into working a total of fourteen years for Rachel. Jacob was now on the receiving end of deceit and trickery. He can now empathize with Esau because he is learning how it feels to find out that someone you trust is readily taking advantage of you for their benefit.

While Jacob was working, he was maturing. No doubt he was taking inventory of his life and his decisions. His decision to steal the blessing deeply strained his relationship with his brother; he would never see his mother or father alive again. The cost of not waiting for God to manifest his promises was high. Even though the cost was high, God was merciful unto Jacob. Jacob encounters God and allows God to change his nature, his character, and after doing so, he would come to realize that God is masterful at taking a mess and making a message. Jacob found that he was no closer to fulfilling the Word of the Lord after all of the deceit and trickery over his life. He was powerless to bring it to pass. Jacob had learned that if God speaks the Word, then God is the one who must make that Word come to pass.

In Isaiah 49:1b (NKJV), the scripture reads, "The Lord has called Me from the womb; From the matrix of My mother He has made mention of My name." In Jeremiah 1:5 (NKJV), God spoke to Jeremiah and said, "Before I formed you in the womb I knew you; Before you were born I sanctified you; I ordained you a prophet to the nations." God calls us by name before He even places us in the womb. He knows our name! In other words, when God had us on His mind, He thought about why He would form us and send us into the world.

Just like Jesus, we have come into the world for a specific purpose. Jeremiah 29:11 (NKJV) says, "For I know the thoughts that I think toward you, …" A thought is an unspoken or an unexpressed word. When God speaks the thought, it becomes a word. That word has the ability and the assignment to become what God intended. Thus, if we paraphrase Isaiah 55:11 to understand man's purpose, we gain a greater insight into who we are. Using Jacob as an example, it might read, "So shall Jacob be that goes forth from My mouth; he shall not return to Me void. But he shall accomplish what I please, and he shall prosper in the thing for which I sent him".

Now replace Jacob's name with yours. We are the expression of the thought of God. He thought about us, and then He spoke us into existence. We cannot return unto Him until we have fulfilled our mission, our purpose, the very thing that He sent us into the earth realm to do. Even though Jacob failed when he used deceit and trickery to try and accomplish the plan and purposes of God, Jacob did not thwart the plans of God. God alone could only turn the mess Jacob had made of his life into something that God could use for His glory.

Jacob worked while he waited for the promise, and at the "set" time, the fullness of time, God sent him back to his brother. Character development took place while he was in hiding. What the devil meant for evil, God used it for His good. (Genesis 50:20) God is powerful enough that He can create a river in the desert, turn mountains into molehills, and a trickster's heart into a righteous one.

What devices have you resorted to when God didn't move when you expected? When God takes too long, do you "assist" Him? When your plans fail, do you grow through the situation? Do you learn more of God in the midst? Or are you doomed to repeat the same mistakes over and over because you will not wait on God to bring His Word to pass?

Prayer

Dear Heavenly Father,

THE GLORY IN WAITING

I bless Your name, and I give You glory, honor, and praise. I worship You in the beauty of holiness, and I declare that there is none like You. You are the one true and living God. Thank you for Your loving kindness and Your tender mercies towards me. Thank you, Lord, for Your thoughts towards me. Thank you for filling me with purpose.

Oh Lord, I have stumbled. I have fallen so short of Your glory. Forgive me. Cleanse me from all unrighteousness. Father, I give myself to You, and I declare that I will fulfill the purpose for which You sent me into the earth to fulfill. I repent for running ahead of You and making a mess. I repent for lagging behind You and refusing to step into destiny. I am grateful that You are the God of another chance. I take that chance right now, and I will do all and be all You desire. I will not return to You void, but I will accomplish the task You sent me here to complete. In Jesus' name, I pray. Amen.

Reflections

THE GLORY IN WAITING

Declaration

I declare that when I wait on Jesus, I will receive everything that He promised. I declare that I am an expression of God's creative mind. I can do all things through Christ, which strengthens me. I declare that, like Jacob, I will work while I wait on God, and I will mature as His child. I will reflect Christ in all of my work so that others will see that He who began the work is finishing the work that He started in me.

CHAPTER 12

The Weight of Waiting

Commit your way to the Lord, Trust also in Him, And He shall bring it to pass.

He shall bring forth your righteousness as the light, And your justice as the noonday. Rest in the Lord, and wait patiently for Him...

PSALM 37:5-7A (NKJV)

In general, waiting is not easy. It requires dependence on someone or something else. Because of the dependence on someone or something, you cannot control how long you will wait, how long you will be delayed, how long you will be passing the time. Even in pregnancy, the woman often is not in control of when the baby will be born. Let's look at that wait for a moment.

Most women do not know the exact moment of conception, even though they may be trying to conceive. The seed is planted in the womb of the woman. Everything the baby needs is in the seed.

The seed requires a certain environment for optimal growth. Pregnancy normally lasts for approximately 40 weeks or nine months. During the first two to three weeks of pregnancy, a woman may not even know that she is pregnant, especially if she does not have any symptoms. However, because the seed is "programmed" for growth, the woman's body will soon begin to let the mother know that she is expecting. Missed cycles, morning sickness, tenderness in her breasts, mood swings, and extreme fatigue are just some of the symptoms a woman may experience as her body begins to adapt to the presence of the "fertilized" seed.

Excited as a woman may be during her first trimester, she cannot rush the process of the child's development. No baby is ready to be born at three months. They are safe in the womb but not yet prepared for the world outside of the womb. So even though the woman may be excited, she must wait for the promise to be manifested. As the baby grows, the woman may need to change her daily routine to accommodate the child's growth.

In the second trimester, the woman's body begins to stretch to allow room for growth. What was previously not visible, others may now begin to see a change. During this trimester, a woman may experience body aches, get stretch marks, and experience swelling. Even though the pregnancy may now be visible, ideally, it is still not time for the baby to be born. More development must take place. The safest and most conducive place for growth is still in the womb.

In the third trimester, the woman's body may experience more symptoms such as shortness of breath, heartburn, swelling in her feet, trouble sleeping, and contractions. The goal is to get as close to 40 weeks as possible to ensure the optimal time for the baby's growth. In pregnancy, you must wait for the promise of the child to be manifested. It is not conducive for the child or the mother to rush the process.

While waiting for the promise to be manifested, preparation takes place. The baby will need a crib or bassinet, bottles, diapers, formula, car seats, carriers, wipes, onesies, blankets, clothes, powder, hooded towels, baby wash, baby shampoo, toys, strollers, etc.

As you get closer to the set time, the appointed time of delivery, anticipation builds. A sign that the wait is about to be over is the breaking of the woman's water. When the water breaks, it's a sign that the baby is getting ready to transition out of the womb. Labor begins. Labor generally means just that. For the promise to be manifested, the mother must now work and push the promise out. The birthing process may be time-consuming, and it may be painful. Some women who have had several babies will describe the birthing process as different for each child. Some mothers and babies may need assistance via a Cesarean section to bring the baby into the world. Either way, whether vaginally or a C-section, the birthing process is not pretty. The image of cuteness does not happen until after the cleaning up of the baby. There may have been tears, sweat, screaming, laughter, threats, a lot of emotions, but at last, the promise has been birthed. The promise is worth the process.

The weight of the wait was not in how much the baby weighed but the mother's need to just let the baby grow.

Oftentimes when we are waiting on God to move, He is moving; we just can't see it yet. Just like the first trimester, the seed has been planted, but the growth is not visible to the naked eye. However, just keep looking at Jesus, and eventually, you will begin to see the change take place. While we are waiting on God, God is waiting on us. His timing is perfect. The Bible declares that when we wait on God, He builds his character in us.

> ³ And not only that, but we also glory in tribulations, knowing that tribulation produces perseverance; ⁴ and perseverance, character; and character, hope. ⁵ Now hope does not disappoint, because the love of God has been poured out in our hearts by the Holy Spirit who was given to us.
>
> Romans 5:3-5 New King James Version (NKJV)

Just as a woman has the responsibility during pregnancy to wait and allow the baby to grow, as believers, we are responsible for being receptive to God's work on the inside of us. Don't fight the process. If you struggle too early in the process, you can suffer a miscarriage. If the timing of conception wasn't right according to your life's schedule or society norms, you might abort the baby.

Life happens at the most opportune and inopportune times. The older generation used to say it this way, if there hasn't been any rain in your life, just wait a while. Rain falls on the just and the unjust. Rain does not have to be negative. God will use that rain to water your seed and cause you to grow up in Him. Just like an acorn contains the blueprint for an oak tree, placed in the right soil and provided the proper nutrients, the acorn will grow into a mighty oak. Likewise, allow the water of the Word of God to help you grow in your walk with the Lord. Don't rush the process.

I don't know many "gluttons for punishment." By that, I mean I don't know many people who enjoy suffering. The reason for waiting is in glorifying the Father. The writer of Hebrews 2:12 (NKJV) wrote, "looking unto Jesus, the author and finisher of our faith, who for the joy that was set before Him endured the cross, despising the shame, and has sat down at the right hand of the throne of God." The reason for going through the tribulations and the trials is the vision that God gave you of the end, of the goal. We go through with grace because He has enabled us to face it. When we face it, He graces every circumstance with His power, love, and wisdom.

Allow Him to develop you through your trials and tribulations. Allow Him to develop your character. When you have done all that you know to do in any given circumstance or situation, wait on God. Expect God to intervene. Expect Him to make the difference. Jesus said in Matthew 11:29-30 (NKJV), "29 Take My yoke upon you and learn from Me, for I am gentle and lowly in heart, and you will find rest for your souls. 30 For My yoke is easy and My burden is light." When we take on the yoke of Jesus and learn of Him, our perspective begins to change. We will see life differently. If being a Christian is a heavy burden, you may be approaching it the wrong way. Undoubtedly, being a Christian has responsibilities, but Jesus said His yoke is easy, and His burden is light. Are you breaking under pressure? Give the burden to Jesus. Are you straining? Give it to Jesus. Depressed? Oppressed? Give it to Jesus. Repressed? Give it to Jesus. His yoke is easy. His burden is light.

Prayer

Dear Heavenly Father,

Sometimes I get frustrated when I don't see You working. Forgive me for being anxious and wanting to rush the process. May I learn that the promise is worth the process. I need to trust You more. I know

You can do it, but honestly, sometimes I feel like You won't do it for me. I sometimes complain that the process is too hard, it's too much, but Jesus said that His yoke is easy.

Father, help me cast off every anxiety, every pressure, and every burden You did not put on me. I recommit my way unto You. I roll my cares over unto You, and I will rest in Your promise. You are not a man that You should lie nor the son of man that You should repent. You are able to keep Your promises to me. Thank you, Father, for Your yoke and Your burden. I choose to wait on You and to rest in Your promises to me. In Jesus' name, I pray. Amen.

Reflections

THE GLORY IN WAITING

Declaration

I declare that the promise is worth the process. I will not run ahead of You oh, Lord, nor will I lag behind You, but I will allow You to order my steps. I choose to obey You even when I cannot see You moving. I declare that I will not allow life's circumstances to beat me down, to depress me, or repress me. I declare that Your yoke is easy, and Your burden is light. I will not be anxious, but I will trust Your Word and rest in You.

CHAPTER 13

Waiting Requires Faith

The Lord is good to those who wait for Him, To the soul who seeks Him.

LAMENTATIONS 3:25 (NKJV)

We sing about Job waiting on the Lord and then describe how the flesh fell off his bones while he waited. Surely a God that would recommend a faithful servant for testing by the devil would not let that servant become emaciated. Or what about when He let Abraham raise the knife to kill Isaac. If Abraham had not been listening to the proceeding Word of God, Isaac might have been a goner. This God cannot be the same God that loved the world so much that He sacrificed His only Son?

The truth of the matter is, we will never fully understand God's thoughts, His ways. Our finite minds cannot handle the greatness of God's infinite wisdom. Isaiah 55:8-9 (NKJV) says, "⁸ For My thoughts are not your thoughts, Nor are your ways My ways," says the Lord. ⁹For as the heavens are higher than the earth, So are My ways higher than your ways, And My thoughts than your thoughts". In other words, God could explain what He is doing, and it would go right over our heads. Why? Because He's God and we are not. That's why this thing called life is a faith walk.

We cannot see air, yet we inhale and exhale without examining each breath to see if it is suitable for our lungs. We expect that when we get up in the morning, we will not be floating, but we will place our feet on the floor. We trust the law of gravity even if we don't understand it. If we can breathe without thinking about each breath before we take it, and if we can trust that we will be grounded and not floating, then we can trust God. It is a faith walk. David said in Psalm 119:105, "Your word is a lamp to my feet, And a light to my path." We cannot see all the way down the road, but God gives us enough light for the next step.

In Psalm 37:23, David states that "The steps of a good man are ordered by the Lord, And He delights in his way." God is delighted when our steps are ordered, established in Him. We can trust that God will guide our footsteps, and He will never lead us astray. And because it is a faith walk, we can trust the Word of the Lord spoken through Jeremiah when he declares that God is good to those that look eagerly for Him, who hope in Him, who expect His goodness, His favor, His grace. God is good. Waiting on the Lord is a good thing. Job was so sure about God that Job put it this way in Job 13:15a (KJV), "Though he slay me, yet will I trust in him." Job felt that waiting on God was better than anything else.

For instance, in Daniel 3:15-18, the Hebrew boys were thrown in the fiery furnace. They declared we don't know if He will deliver us or not, but we know that He can do so. If we die believing Him, we have lost nothing and gained everything because He is trustworthy. We may not be able to see it or understand it, but we can trust Him with our lives. The writer of Hebrews in chapter 11:13 (NKJV) talks of the biblical heroes of faith, including Abraham and Sarah, David, Samson, and Rahab. Of these, they "all died in faith, not having received the promises, but having seen them afar off were assured of them, embraced *them,* and confessed that they were strangers and pilgrims on the earth." The list is full of imperfect people believing, trusting, hoping in, and waiting on a perfect God. That same verse in the Amplified Classic Bible says,

> [13] These people all died controlled *and* sustained by their faith, but not having received the tangible fulfillment of [God's] promises, only having seen it *and* greeted it from a great distance by faith, and all the while acknowledging *and* confessing that they were strangers *and* temporary residents *and* exiles upon the earth."

Whether you see the fulfillment of His promises to you on earth or you receive the fulfillment in Heaven, God rewards those who wait on Him with goodness. If you trust Him, He will not fail you. He's just that good. He's just that consistent, that faithful.

We are made in the image of God, in His character, in His likeness. If we indeed have His attributes, then we are also able to be faithful. God requires faith as the down payment on anything that we hope for. Hebrews 11:6 (NKJV) states, "[6]But without faith it is impossible to please Him, for he who comes to God must believe that He is, and that He is a rewarder of those who diligently seek Him". In this passage, the Greek word for "diligently" is *ekzēteō*, which means seek after, seek carefully, inquire, require, seek out or investigate.

God rewards those who are assertive in their faith. He rewards those who are seeking after Him, investigating, enquiring, or asking of Him. Suffice it to say, God can do anything. He doesn't need our help to rule or dominate this world. However, He has chosen us to be His partners, His image-bearers in the earth, to reflect Him properly; we must operate in faith.

God rewards those who are **"not"** passive in their faith. In other words, we must believe that He exists and that He hears us and will reward those who diligently seek Him. First John 3:22 (NKJV) states, "And whatever we ask we receive from Him, because we keep His commandments and do those things that are pleasing in His sight." We see that we receive from Him through our obedience to Him and by doing things pleasing in His sight. However, if we are not obedient or doing things contrary to God's will, we should not expect to receive anything from the Lord. James 1:6-8 (NKJV) explains:

> [6]But let him ask in faith, with no doubting, for he who doubts is like a wave of the sea driven and tossed by the wind. [7] For let not that man suppose that he will receive anything from the Lord; [8] he is a double-minded man, unstable in all his ways.

We must live our lives controlled and sustained by faith if we want to please the Lord. Faith pleases God. If we are anxious, doubtful, and unbelieving, we cannot expect that He will move on our behalf; He is not obligated to. Why? Because the contract between man and God requires faith on our part. We can surmise then that waiting on God requires faith in God, and if we wait in faith, He will hear us and answer us. Hallelujah, we can wait in faith, believing that when we pray to Him, He hears us and is ready and able to move on our behalf.

Prayer

Dear Heavenly Father,

I come to You with a grateful heart, thanking you for Your faithfulness towards me. Father, I am grateful that You chose to partner with mankind in the earth realm and promised to hear us and help those of us who are in the right relationship with You. Forgive us, Lord, for being unfaithful and for being faithless. God, sometimes we have become impatient in waiting on You, and we have wavered in our faith. God, Your Word declares that we should not expect to receive anything from You if we waver.

Have mercy on us, oh Lord, according to Your tender mercies and Your loving kindness. Blot out our transgressions. Restore to us the joy of our salvation. Cause us to remember Your faithfulness and to count You faithful. May we renew our minds and renew our vow of faithfulness to You. We trust You, God, to keep Your Word. Have Your way in our hearts, in our minds, in our lives, and may we be pleasing to You, oh Lord, in Jesus' name we pray. Amen.

Reflections

THE GLORY IN WAITING

Declaration

I declare that You are a faithful God. I declare that because You are faithful, I have the ability to be faithful. I choose to believe Your Word and apply it to every circumstance and situation in my life. I declare that I will wait in expectation that You will work on my behalf. I declare that by the power of God, I am able to wait in faith without wavering. Yes, I am confident that You are able to do exceedingly, abundantly above all that I can ask, think, hope, or imagine. As I keep my contract with You, I declare that You, Father God, are faithful to keep your Word to me. I declare that I will not move ahead of You or lag behind You, but I will listen to Your voice and march to Your beat. I declare that you are positioning me for my breakthrough, and I will be ready to receive in Jesus' name.

CHAPTER 14

Set Time

You will arise and have mercy on Zion; For the time to favor her, Yes, the set time, has come.

PSALM 102:13 (NKJV)

The ancient Greeks used three words to define time: Chronos, Aion, Kairos. Chronos is the passage or duration of time. It is the time we count; it's reflected in the hourglass, the sundial, a watch, a stopwatch. When you ask, "what time is it?" You are usually looking for a numerical response such as, "it's 5:45". Aion is a long period of time, like an era or epoch. It is the root from which we get the word, eon. Kairos is sometimes defined as season, but it is also defined as an opportunity or opportune moment, the right time. Let's specifically look at Chronos and Kairos.

Chronos is quantitative in nature, while Kairos is qualitative in nature. Chronos can be divided into seconds, minutes, hours, days, and so forth. Kairos may be numerical in that a season may last three months, but the weather may vary such that one would say it feels like summer when, in fact, the calendar (Chronos) says it is winter.

We often miss the Kairos of God because we did not value the Chronos. God has given us time as a tool to assist us in fulfilling our purpose. When we don't properly use time, we abuse it. Myles Monroe taught us that if the purpose of a thing is not known, then abuse (abnormal use) is inevitable. If you do not understand why God gave us time, then abuse of the tool will be the result. Galatians 4:4 (KJV) states, "But when the fullness of the time had come, God sent forth His Son, born of a woman, born under the law." This scripture says when the right time had come, or more specifically at the exact opportune time, Christ was born.

How do we know it was the right time? God had orchestrated the birth of Jesus, foretold through 55 prophecies in the Old Testament. At the right time (chronologically), Jesus was born. If you can imagine an hourglass, the sand is slowly draining from one end to the other, and it was at the exact moment that the last grain had fallen into the bottom of the hourglass that Jesus was born. Jesus fulfilling just eight of the prophecies is a statistical improbability! He didn't just fulfill eight. He fulfilled every prophecy that predicted his birth, life, death, and resurrection. There are instances or moments that are set. If you miss the time, you have missed the opportunity.

Look at what Mark wrote in Mark 1:14-15 (NKJV), "[14] Now after John was put in prison, Jesus came to Galilee, preaching the gospel of the kingdom of God, [15] and saying, "The time is fulfilled, and the kingdom of God is at hand. Repent, and believe in the gospel." Jesus was saying, the time that was preordained in the heavens is now, it's the right time, the right season for me to come preaching the good news of the kingdom of God. It was not happenstance or coincidental. His arrival was fixed and definite; it was the opportune time.

Have you ever noticed that when the National Aeronautics and Space Administration (NASA) is preparing a rocket to go into outer space, they calculate the window of time? If they are unable to launch due to weather or technological issues, the mission is delayed until another appropriate time. Likewise, there are times when we must be obedient to God and launch when He tells us to, or we may create a mess or miss our opportunity altogether.

In Ecclesiastes 3:1(NKJV), Solomon wrote, "To everything there is a season, A time for every purpose under heaven." Everything has a set or appointed season of time. Everything has an opportune moment for its purpose to be realized under heaven. Have you ever noticed that some of your relationships just seemed to click like clockwork? You meet by accident or incident, and there is an immediate connection. You recognize the "specialness" of the moment. That's an appointed meeting, a Kairos happening. In relationships, some of you move too fast, others too slow. As a result, you cannot seem to get the right timing for the relationship to work out.

What am I saying? God made us creatures of free will. We are not robots; we have a choice. Joshua speaking to the children of Israel in Joshua 24:15, put it this way:

> "And if it seem evil unto you to serve the LORD, choose you this day whom ye will serve; whether the gods which your fathers served that were on the other side of the flood, or the gods of the Amorites, in

whose land ye dwell: but as for me and my house, we
will serve the LORD.

Everybody decides to serve or not to serve the Lord. If you say,
I've never made that decision, or I don't intend to make a conscious
decision, your indecision was a decision. Jesus in Revelation 3:16
would rather that you be cold or hot. Lukewarm folk will be spewed
out of the mouth of God. Lukewarm people are distasteful to God.
He created man with the ability to think and actively choose
salvation or damnation.

Damnation can look, taste, smell, feel, sound like heaven, which
is more accurately described as the pleasures of sin or the passing or
temporary nature of sin. Don't make a permanent decision about a
temporary season in your life. For instance, marriage is a lifetime
commitment. Don't get locked into a contract with someone
because you were afraid of being alone and lonely. If the motive is
wrong, the outcome will be wrong. You cannot get God's results
using Satan's methods. It just doesn't work like that.

God has a set time and an appointed place for your blessing.
You must be diligent in following all His directions if you want to
get His results. God told Abraham to take Isaac up the mountain and
to sacrifice him. Abraham raised the knife to slay the promised son,
and it was then that God told him not to harm the child. He hears
the ram that is stuck in the thicket and sacrifices the ram unto God.
When did the ram get caught in the thicket? I believe it was the
moment Abraham obeyed God by going up to the mountain with
Isaac. If Abraham had gone to another mountain or anywhere else
that he wanted to go, he would not have been in the appointed place
at the appointed time.

Chronos will not dictate your set time, your Kairos moment, or season, but it will facilitate it. What do I mean? Let's look at Jesus and his mother, Mary. In John chapter 2, Jesus and his disciples attend a wedding at Cana. His mother comes to Him and tells Him that they have run out of wine. Jesus asks Mary, "What do you want me to do about it? My time is not yet come." In other words, the definite time or season has not started yet; the Kairos is not yet. His mother's response may seem odd to some, but it is exactly what we need to learn. She heard what He said, and then she turned to the servants and said, "Whatever, He tells you to do, do it." She responded in faith because she had made a request of Him. Her faith moved the Kairos into action. Because of her faith, Jesus performed his first miracle, and it was at a wedding.

Faith moves the timepiece of Heaven. Faith will enact a Kairos moment that Chronos can only facilitate; it cannot dominate. If you don't like the season you are in, change it. Bust a faith move and watch God enter your Chronos and change it into Kairos moment, a time when God intervenes in your life.

Chronos should not dominate your life. It is a tool to help you always operate in the Kairos of God. We should be moving from Kairos to Kairos.

Examine yourself. What issues with time do you have? Are you missing the Kairos of God because you are only focused on the Chronos? God has a set time for favor, for deliverance, for healing, for providing that undeniable, irrefutable blessing upon your life. What is keeping you out of your Kairos? Are you truly waiting on God, or is He waiting on you?

Prayer

Dear Heavenly Father,

Thank you for the gift of time. I repent because I know that I do not always treat time as a gift. I am often not purposeful in my use of time, so I miss precious opportunities to be used by You. My emotions get the best of me, and I lash out in frustration when situations governed by Chronos, by the clock, are affecting me negatively.

Father, I want to be in sync with You. Moving when you tell me to move but standing still when You tell me to stand. Help me to understand Your gift of time. My desire is to grow from Kairos to Kairos in You. I trust you, God. Where my impatience is my own doing, teach me how to wait so that in the "fulness of time," Your will and purpose will be manifested in my life. In Jesus' name. Amen.

Reflections

THE GLORY IN WAITING

Declaration

I declare that I am wise in my use of time. I will not lag behind or run ahead of God in this next season, but I willingly allow God to order my steps. I declare that I listen for His voice and will not follow another, not even my own. I declare that this next season is a season of victory for me in Christ Jesus, for He has already made me the victor.

I declare that I will be like Abraham and listen for Father's instructions so that if He calls me to sacrifice that thing that is most precious to me, I can trust Him to have a ram in the bush for me. I declare that God is worth the wait, and I trust Him while I am waiting.

CHAPTER 15

The Cost of Impatience

Therefore, I felt compelled, and offered a burnt offering.

1 SAMUEL 13:12B (NKJV)

Sometimes, we just will not wait for God to move. God tells us what He is going to do. We rejoice; we are excited. When we don't understand His timing, we start to doubt. We doubt our ability to hear Him, and we doubt His ability to fix it for us. Proverbs 13:12 (NKJV) says, "Hope deferred makes the heart sick, but when the desire is fulfilled, it is a tree of life." Have you been waiting for something or someone so long that your heart aches about the situation? Maybe your spouse is addicted to drugs, your children are rebellious, or your supervisor refuses to promote you but continues to give you all the work. Maybe the wait feels like it's taking forever because you are more focused on what time it is rather than you are on working while you wait.

Have you ever called someone, and you could not reach them when you expected to? The more you called and didn't get an answer, the more concerned you became, the more concerned you became, the more it felt like time was standing still. You became frantic, and by the time they responded, you were in a full panic attack or a full meltdown mode. They had no idea why you were so frantic. When you ask them why they didn't answer your call, their response might have been, "My phone died, and I wasn't aware of it until I tried to call you," or "I was in a meeting, and I put my phone on silent mode. We just got out of the meeting."

You realized that your emotions had run amok and disturbed your peace. Anxiety built up, emotions and imagination ran wild, and now you are exhausted, all because of impatience. You were not willing, or felt like you were not able, to wait.

Science tells us that when we become impatient, neurologically, our prefrontal cortex switches off. The prefrontal cortex is the area responsible for high-level thinking. When that area is switched off, the amygdala takes over. The hormones that control stress start rising, causing emotions such as anger, anxiety, and irritability to set in. As we start feeling these intense emotions, our bodies overload our brain with signals that appear to distort our sense of time. A couple of minutes of worry can feel like 30 minutes or more.

In the fairytale, *Snow White and the Seven Dwarfs*, Snow White sings "Whistle While You Work" to pass the time while she and the forest animals are cleaning the house. Work may be labor-intensive, but you can do so with a song in your heart. When you approach work with a different attitude, you can achieve a lot with a melody in your heart. You often will go further than you realize because you stopped focusing on the task.

THE GLORY IN WAITING

Likewise, when we are waiting on someone or something, if we would worship God in the process, we may find that when "the wait" does not preoccupy our thoughts, anxiety, doubt, or worry cannot establish a foothold and destroy our peace of mind. Often you will see people exercising with earbuds in their ears. They are listening either to music or to motivational teaching. They might even be on the phone talking to someone while they walk or run. Why is that important? The distraction helps one complete the task because the individual does not focus on the time or discomfort.

If King Saul had focused on something other than people-pleasing, he might have remained the king of Israel. Instead, he chose disobedience and impatience, and God rejected him as the king. It is never okay to disobey God. It is never okay to take matters into your own hands because you got tired of waiting on God. If we called Sarah to the witness stand, she might urge you not to move ahead of God. Otherwise, your actions may birth something that will mock the promise of God in your life.

When you are impatient, you are irritable or restless, and you may be frustrated, agitated, or nervous. Impatient people will drive erratically, zigging and zagging, trying to speed to their destination. Sometimes, their actions result in an accident. Other times, no matter how much they zigged and zagged, they did not get to their destination any faster. They expended more energy, but they did not achieve their goal.

James 1:4 says, "But let patience have *its* perfect work, that you may be perfect and complete, lacking nothing." Let patience rule you; let patience mature you so that you can grow and lack nothing spiritually or emotionally. It takes discipline to grow in patience. Paul said in 2 Corinthians 10:5 to cast down every imagination that exalts itself against the knowledge of God. You must take your thoughts captive, and when you do, you can begin to exert peace where fear and anxiety was in control. You can exert joy where sorrow had built a nest. You may ask, how do I do this? You do it through the power of prayer. Pray and then obey. Pray and then obey. PRAY AND THEN OBEY.

In 1 Samuel 13, we see how impatience can cause us to act foolishly. The Philistines had gathered to fight against Israel. The odds numerically were not in Israel's favor as they were outnumbered 10 to 1. Samuel had told King Saul to wait seven days, and he would come and offer a sacrifice unto the Lord. When the Israelites saw they were outnumbered, they were afraid. They were so afraid that many of them ran and hid in caves, in thickets, in rocks, in holes, and in pits. Some even crossed over the Jordan.

The ones that stayed with King Saul were trembling. The people did not have any faith in themselves, and they certainly had forgotten about the God they served. When King Saul saw his troops scattering and noted that Samuel had not come in seven days like he said, Saul took matters into his own hands. He offered the burnt offering. King Saul decided that he would do the task set aside for the priests and prophets to do.

How many times have you responded like King Saul? God tells you to do something a certain way, and when He doesn't respond when you believe He should, you take matters into your own hands. As soon as he disobeyed God, Samuel showed up and asked King Saul, "What have you done?" Saul proceeds to explain to Samuel that the people were scattering, and he was late getting there, so he "felt compelled." Other versions say that King Saul "forced" himself." The word in Hebrew translated forced or compelled is *aphaq*. This word in other verses is translated, "to hold, be strong, restrain, hold back." Isn't that interesting? The same word that is translated to restrain or hold back can also be translated to force or compel oneself. What am I saying? The pressure to do something was internal, not external. King Saul could have compelled himself (refrained from acting out of turn) to wait until Samuel arrived but instead of refraining himself, he had the "can't help its." In other words, he had the ability to resist the urge, but he chose to give in to it. Sound familiar?

King Saul had gotten into the habit of doing things his way and then trying to pass off his disobedience and impatience as righteousness. In 1 Samuel 15:18-19, the prophet Samuel is talking to King Saul and asks him, "[18]Now the Lord sent you on a mission, and said, 'Go, and utterly destroy the sinners, the Amalekites, and fight against them until they are consumed.' [19]Why then did you not obey the voice of the Lord?" Saul responds with excuses for why he disobeyed God.

Do not develop the habit of half obedience. Half obedience is full disobedience. If you fail to wait on God, do not expect Him to bless your mess. God is looking for someone who will move in faith and trust Him to work on their behalf even when they cannot see Him moving. Saul's impatience cost him the kingdom. What has your impatience cost you?

Prayer

Dear Heavenly Father,

Forgive me, oh Lord, for being impatient and not waiting on You. I have the ability to wait, to be patient, but sometimes I just don't want to. I must admit, I don't know how much my impatience has cost me. Father, I pray that my impatience has not brought harm or injury to another. Father, only You can take my mess and get glory out of it. Father, get the glory in spite of me. Help me, oh God. I want to grow in faith and in patience and let patience have her perfect work in me.

Father, I pray that I will learn to worship you while I am waiting. Focus my heart, Lord. Your Word says in Proverbs 21:1 that you hold the king's heart in your hand and that you can turn it whatever way that you wish. Please turn my heart towards You. If my heart is stony, please remove it and give me a heart of flesh. May disobedience become distasteful to me, and obedience become pleasurable. Father, I know that You have forgiven me, and I thank you now for a fresh start in You. I love You, and I desire to please You, Lord. In Jesus' name, I pray. Amen.

Reflections

THE GLORY IN WAITING

Declaration

I declare that I will wait on the Lord. I will trust the Lord with my whole heart. I declare that I will no longer lean on my own intellect and understanding, but I will have faith in God. I declare that I will not let my eye gate get me in trouble. I declare that if I can't see my way out, I trust God to make a way out of no way. I declare that I trust God. God's track record is good. He has not failed yet. God's credit with me is good. I declare that I will wait until the Lord shows up, and I will not be moved by the circumstance nor the people. I declare that my eyes are on the Lord, and my ears are attuned to His voice. I declare that I am patient.

CHAPTER 16

Procrastination

The Psalmist cried out, "So teach us to number our days, that we may apply our hearts to wisdom."

PSALMS 90:12 (NKJV)

Have you ever had a project, and the due date was several months away, and when you saw the requirements, you responded, "I've got time, no worries?" What about preparing for an important social gathering or banquet, and when you start out that morning to run your errands, you think, *I have plenty of time to do all I need to do before I need to get dressed for the evening.* Then something happens. The car gets a flat tire, the store is crowded, there's only one cashier, the line is long. Before you know it, time has gotten away from you, and you no longer have the safety net of time. You are now running late. What happened?

James 4:17 says, "Therefore, to him who knows to do good and does not do it, to him it is sin." News flash: Procrastination is a sin. I said it, and I'm not taking it back. Procrastination is not your friend; procrastination is a sin. If God told you to do something and you have not done it, your delayed obedience is a sin. Colossians 3:6 states that the wrath of God comes upon the sons of disobedience. To be clear, it is not okay for you or for me to be cavalier, careless, inconsiderate, or lazy about obeying God. Procrastination will have you out of the will of God and out of position in the body of Christ.

Some mistakes and poor decisions can be avoided if we are where we should be. Let's look at an example of a domino effect of being out of position. In 2 Samuel 11:1, the text said that it was the time of year when kings go out to battle. Why is King David laying up in his palace if the kings have gone out to battle? For whatever reason, King David procrastinated, was out of position, and did not go into battle. If King David had gone out to battle as the other kings did, he:

- would not have seen Bathsheba bathing. If he had not seen Bathsheba bathing,
- would not have lusted,
- would not have betrayed his mighty man of valor once he was told that Bathsheba was Uriah's wife
- would not have sent for Bathsheba,
- would not have caused her to sin against her husband by laying with her,
- would not have gotten her pregnant,
- would not have sent for her husband under false pretenses, and when Uriah would not take the bait and sleep with his wife because his troops were still fighting
- would not have involved others in his sin by ordering them to cover up his sinful actions

- would not have devised a plot and had a faithful and loyal soldier killed.
- would not have had to bury his son, who died because of David's sin.

The domino effect of willful sin is costly. 1 John 3:4 (AMPC) says, everyone who commits (practices) sin is guilty of lawlessness; for [that is what] sin is, lawlessness (the breaking, violating of God's law by transgression or neglect—being unrestrained and unregulated by His commands and His will). David became unrestrained and unregulated. He was not sensitive to the Spirit. As believers in the Lord Jesus Christ, we should not be practicing sin.

Jesus forgives, but He also holds us accountable for our thoughts, actions, and inactions. We ought to repent every time we cast off what Jesus told us to do because His request was not convenient, made us feel uncomfortable, or challenged us. Obedience just may save your life or the life of someone you know. Disobedience may cost you or someone you know. If King David had only been in position....

Paul, in his first letter to the Corinthians, stated that everything should be done decently and in order. God is a God of order. Procrastination causes disruptions and disorder in a person's life. Be of good courage: If you confess your sin, your procrastination, your delayed obedience, God is faithful to forgive you and cleanse you. Then you can follow Paul's admonition in Ephesians 5:15-16 to walk circumspectly, not as a fool but as a wise person who can redeem the time. God will enable you to redeem, convert your lazy, procrastinating behavior into righteous behavior that will bring Him glory.

There is an old adage that states, "don't put off until tomorrow what you can do today." Psalm 119:60 (NKJV) says, "I made haste, and did not delay to keep Your commandments." We need to develop a habit of obeying God as soon as He speaks to us. We get in a hurry for things we want -- that sale at the mall, dinner at our favorite restaurant, or going to the movies with our friends. Why can't we get in a hurry to do God's work?

What are you waiting for? Why are you delaying moving in the things of God? Are you afraid of failure, or are you afraid of success? Are you delaying because you don't know how to do what God requires or don't believe that you are worthy or capable of doing what He asked?

Gideon did not see himself as a mighty man of valor, yet God had predestined him to be a deliverer for Israel. Ignorance of what to do is not an excuse for doing nothing. James says in James 1:5 that if we lack wisdom, we should ask God, who willingly gives us His insight.

Don't miss the Kairos of God because you are in a state of disobedience. Choose to live a life in obedience to God's will and His way. Choose to obey. God will help you be your best authentic self, but you must first yield. Managing our time is necessary if we are going to be successful in all that God has given us to do. If God has given you an assignment, ask Him how to do it, ask Him for the resources, ask Him for the insight. Ask Him! He's waiting on you!

Prayer

Dear Heavenly Father,

THE GLORY IN WAITING

Please forgive me. I repent for procrastinating in the things that You have told me to do. I come to You acknowledging that I have procrastinated and dragged my feet when it came to obeying You. I didn't want to fail You, so I ended up doing nothing. I didn't believe that You chose me for the assignment, and I allowed unbelief to be as cement that had me locked in position, unable to move. After a while, I was no longer responding to the conviction of the Holy Spirit, but now I was wallowing in condemnation because I heard You when You gave the assignment, and I didn't respond.

Father, I realize that some opportunities may not come back around as I have missed the opportune time. However, God, I know that You are the God of the breakthrough, the God of another chance. Give me another chance to obey You, to honor You with my obedience. I realize You will not require anything of me that You cannot provide the resources to accomplish. I changed my perception, and instead of looking at things through the lens of "I can't," Father, I chose to do all things through Christ who strengthens me. Thank you, Lord. In Jesus' name, I pray. Amen.

Reflections

THE GLORY IN WAITING

Declaration

I declare that I will not put off doing what God has called me to do. I declare that I will manage my time wisely. I am confident that He who began a good work in me is faithful to complete it. I refuse to disobey God by delaying my response to His instructions. I declare that I can do all things through Christ who strengthens me. I declare that I am organized and efficient. I declare that I have the wisdom to do all that God commands of me. I will study to show myself approved unto God. I declare that I am delivered from the spirit of procrastination. The Spirit of God has set me free. I declare that I will not leave this earth until I have fulfilled in excellence every assignment God has given me.

CHAPTER 17

Glory

to which He called you by our gospel, for the obtaining
of the glory of our Lord Jesus Christ.

2 THESSALONIANS 2:14 (NKJV)

What is glory, and why is it important? The Hebrew word for glory
is kavod. Kavod is translated as importance, weight, deference, or
heaviness. It also means respect, honor, and majesty. In Exodus
40:34-35, Moses writes: "34Then the cloud covered the tabernacle of
meeting, and the glory of the Lord filled the tabernacle. 35And
Moses was not able to enter the tabernacle of meeting, because the
cloud rested above it, and the glory of the Lord filled the tabernacle".
In this passage, the glory was described as a visible cloud. This cloud
didn't just stay in the sky, but it came down and filled the tent that
had been dedicated to the service of God. God blessed the place with
His tangible, visible presence.

In simplest terms, the kavod, the glory of God, is His visible or
manifested presence. When we talk about His manifested presence,

we are saying that the invisible God is now visible to us. The invisible God is now knowable. Another way to express the glory of God would be to say that it is the character of God made visible. Paul, in his letter to the Colossians, said this:

> ⁶As ye have therefore received Christ Jesus the Lord, so walk ye in him:

> ⁷Rooted and built up in him, and stablished in the faith, as ye have been taught, abounding therein with thanksgiving. ⁸Beware lest any man spoil you through philosophy and vain deceit, after the tradition of men, after the rudiments of the world, and not after Christ. ⁹For in him dwelleth all the fulness of the Godhead bodily.

> Colossians 2:6-9 (KJV)

Jesus is the visible expression of the Father, Son, and Holy Spirit. Before we accepted His gift of life in exchange for our death sentence, we were not worthy of God. Romans 3:23 states, "for all have sinned and fall short of the glory of God." If we fall short of his tangible presence, how can we reflect Him? We can reflect Him because we have our very existence in Christ. Our lives are hidden in Christ. Paul shares in 2 Corinthians 5:17 (NKJV), "Therefore, if anyone is in Christ, he is a new creation; old things have passed away; behold, all things have become new."

If I am a new creation, why do I need to wait on God? What is the reason for waiting? Don't I have His presence? We wait on God because we are daily being changed into His image. Our thought patterns must conform to the Word of God. Paul said in Romans 12:1-2 that we should present our bodies as a living sacrifice. We should allow God to use us whenever, for as long as He wants to. The sacrifice is transformed in the fire. What went on the altar as flesh and blood is consumed by the fire. The flesh no longer controls the movement; the spirit does. "Being confident of this very thing, that He who has begun a good work in you will complete it until the day of Jesus Christ"(Philippians 1:6 NKJV).

In the New Testament, the Greek word most often translated to glory is doxa. Doxa means glory, splendor, and honor. Jesus is the glory of the Father (Hebrews 1:3), and we are the glory of the Son (John 17:10). As we spend time in God's presence, we begin to look more and more like Him. We can be confident that every sacrifice, every trial, every tribulation will work for our good. His visible presence, His shekinah glory settles upon us, and our flaws fade as His glory shines through. Because we have His Holy Spirit in us, when people look at us, they should see the glory of God shining through us. We are to let our light shine so that men will see the good works and glorify the Father. Let means to permit, to allow. If the world does not see Jesus when they look at us, we are not weighty enough with His presence. His presence is heavy; it covers, it delivers, it sets captives free.

In the first chapter of Acts, we see the beginnings of a fledgling church. The disciples were stepping into something new, something different, something other than anything they had experienced before. There was no workbook or manual for them to refer to. The Word of God had come to earth in the form of a man named Jesus, and He flipped the script on everything that they thought they knew about God. After His resurrection, Jesus stayed for 40 days before ascending into Heaven. He commanded them not to depart from Jerusalem but to wait for the Comforter to come! In this passage, the

THE GLORY IN WAITING

Greek word for wait is perimenō, which means to stay around, await. Literally, Jesus told them, do not go anywhere but physically stay there in Jerusalem. The promise of the Comforter, the Holy Spirit, was tied to a place and a time.

The disciples gathered together in the upper room, and they prayed. While praying, they all began to get on the same wavelength. They achieved unity and were on one accord through prayer and supplication. Ten days later, after He ascended and the day of Pentecost had "fully come," the Holy Spirit entered the upper room where they were praying and waiting and filled all who were there with His spirit. Do you see the importance of waiting? Power is received as a result of waiting. They loved God and wanted to please Him, but they needed the indwelling of the Holy Spirit in order to have the power, the ability to reflect Jesus to the world. The glory of God was no longer just resting upon man but was now emanating from within man.

The glory in waiting is this: we reflect God to the world. We are able to reflect God to the world because we have the Holy Spirit residing inside of us. If the world wants to see God, they can look at us. If we wait on God, if we serve Him with our whole heart, if we work and do His pleasure, we will reflect His glory for all to see, and we will demonstrate that He was worth the wait. Because the disciples waited for the Promise, they had the power to change and affect the whole world for Christ. Think about it, they didn't have any telephones, no fax machines, no television, no computers, and no electronics, yet they revolutionized their world with the gospel of Jesus Christ! How? They reflected Him in their lifestyles, in their ministry, and in their families.

THE GLORY IN WAITING

There is a reward in living your life for Christ. If you wait on the Lord, you will reap a harvest. There is glory in waiting. Wait, I say, on the Lord. He is worth the wait.

Prayer

Dear Heavenly Father,

Thank you for the gift of Your Son. Thank you for the Holy Spirit. Thank you for giving us everything pertaining to life and godliness. Thank you for entrusting us with Your glory. Even when we fell short of Your glory, You provided the means by which we would be restored to glory. Thank you, Father, for Your mercy and Your grace. You are an awesome Daddy, and we worship You. You are God alone. None can be compared to You.

I pray that we will reflect You in our thoughts, words, deeds, and actions every day. May the world see You when they look at us. We bear Your image. We are Your reflection. May we hide Your Word in our hearts so that we will not sin against You. Father, may we study to show ourselves approved that we won't have to be ashamed because we have rightly divided the Word of God.

Father, You are worth the wait. May we be ever mindful that if You spoke it, then You have the ability to bring it to pass—whatever "it" is! Father, there is a glory in waiting for You. We are honored to serve You, humbled to know You, thankful to love You. We will reflect Your glory whenever and wherever we go in Jesus' name. Amen.

Reflections

THE GLORY IN WAITING

Declaration

I declare that God is worth the wait. I declare that I will not rush God, nor will I lag behind, but like the disciples on the day of Pentecost, I will be in one accord with the Spirit of God. I declare that I am an image-bearer. I bear the image of Christ. I reflect His glory at all times. I declare that I do not take breaks from being in His presence.

I love God, and because I love Him, I keep His commandments, and I represent God well. When the world sees me, they see Christ. When acquaintances see me, they see Christ. When my family and loved ones see me, they see Christ. When I look in the mirror of the Word of God, I see Christ. I am a manifestation of God in the earth realm. I am a designated representative of the one true and living God. I declare that my thoughts, words, deeds, and actions will reflect God. I declare that I will fulfill my purpose on this earth as I will be all and do all that God sent me here to do.

Made in the USA
Las Vegas, NV
14 September 2024

95257668R00095